The View from the Border

The View from the Border

Why Catholics Leave the Church and Why They Stay

John N. Kotre

with a new introduction by the author

AldineTransaction
A Division of Transaction Publishers
New Brunswick (U.S.A.) and London (U.K.)

New material this edition 2009
Copyright © 1971 by John N. Kotre.

All rights reserved under International and Pan-American Copyright
Conventions. No part of this book may be reproduced or transmitted in
any form or by any means, electronic or mechanical, including photocopy,
recording, or any information storage and retrieval system, without prior
permission in writing from the publisher. All inquiries should be addressed
to AldineTransaction, A Division of Transaction Publishers, Rutgers—The
State University, 35 Berrue Circle, Piscataway, New Jersey 08854-8042.
www.transactionpub.com

This book is printed on acid-free paper that meets the American National
Standard for Permanence of Paper for Printed Library Materials.

Library of Congress Catalog Number: 2008031216
ISBN: 978-0-202-36307-3
Printed in the United States of America

Library of Congress Cataloging-in-Publication Data

Kotre, John N.
  The view from the border : why Catholics leave the church and why
they stay / John N. Kotre ; with a new introduction by the author.
      p. cm.
  Includes bibliographical references and index.
  ISBN 978-0-202-36307-3 (alk. paper)
      1. Christian sociology—Catholic Church--Statistics. 2. Christi-
anity—Psychology—Statistics.   I. Title.

BT738.K68 2008
282'.73—dc22
                                                      2008031216

To Ann Marie

Contents

Part IV: Extensions

Acknowledgments

The nature of this study made me especially dependent upon those with whom it is concerned. Not only did persons have to agree to spend several hours of their time being interviewed, they had to be a means of locating the next subject, a link in a chain whose end point I did not know. Sometimes there were in existence many links extending from subjects just interviewed to ones yet to be contacted. At other times I was down to the last possible link. That the chain was never broken was due to the resourcefulness of the one hundred people whom this study is about and their sympathy for a fellow graduate student. To them I am primarily indebted.

Backing up the other side—my side—of the observer-observed dyad were a number of competent and helpful people. Father Andrew Greeley of the National Opinion Research Center made important suggestions at critical points and, in general, helped to move the study along. Milton Rosenberg, Jacob Getzels, and Brewster Smith, all of the Department of Psychology at the University of Chicago, read the manuscript in various stages and gave encouraging feedback. Much of the painstaking key-punching and data analysis was handled flawlessly by Kathy Kennedy, my student assistant at Lake Forest College. My wife Ann Marie helped in numerous ways, coding and tabulating data, editing and typing the final manuscript. Fran Kotre, Steve Padover, Jon Finkle-stein, Margery Dorn, and Margery Lundh, too, all provided assistance of various kinds along the way.

Expenses for duplication of the questionnaire, location of subjects, and data analysis were borne by the Department of Psychology at the University of Chicago. Part of the time I worked on this project I was supported by a United States Public Health Service Traineeship in Social Psychology (Grant No. 5 T1 MH–07090–08).

To all who were of help, I extend my thanks.

Introduction to the
Transaction Edition

The God wars are raging once again. A band of neo-atheists—Richard Dawkins, Daniel Dennett, Sam Harris, Christopher Hitchens, and others—are on a mission to end the "God delusion" once and for all. Back in the late 1960s, when I was doing the research for this book, "death-of-God" theologians were also trying to bury the Almighty. (Yes, they were *theologians*.) Harvey Cox had proclaimed—and celebrated—"the loosing of the world from religion and quasi-religious understandings of itself." Thomas Altizer and William Hamilton had been blunter: "We must realize that the death of God is an historical event, that God has died in our cosmos, in our history, in our *existenz*." To judge from the state of our *existenz* in 2008, God must have missed his obituary.

I've often wondered how data in *The View from the Border* would inform today's debate. Daniel Dennett might use the idiom of "breaking the spell" to describe the book's subject matter; that at least is the title of one of his books. He might applaud the fact that this was a scientific study, for science is how he wants to break religion's spell. But *The View from the Border* shows that breaking from religion, or remaining part of it, isn't about spells at all. It isn't about reason, science or "evidence." Rather, it's about the

xi

whole of a life, about trust and betrayal, about anger and joy, about loneliness and friendship, about awe and curiosity. It's about parents and lovers and children. It's about the intellect too, but something comes before intellect, some a-rational starting point, some pre-intellectual desire.

In 2008 the Pew Forum's *U.S. Religious Landscape Survey* reported that 28 percent of American adults had left the faith of their childhood—44 percent, if you included movement among Protestant denominations. *The View from the Border* addresses Catholic attrition, which was the greatest of all. The subjects of the book were a hundred young adults aged 21-31. By anyone's definition they were among the best and the brightest products of Catholic education. Fifty, by their own definition, were still *in* the church. Fifty were *out*. Their early exposure to Catholicism had been identical. Both Ins and Outs had attended Mass every Sunday, and about half of each group reported prolonged periods of attendance at weekday Masses. Most of each group experienced sixteen full years of Catholic education. Most said that being a Catholic had been "one of the three most important things in my life." Yet in their twenties they went separate ways.

From April to December of 1968 I stood at the border, a 400-item questionnaire in hand, and observed them staying or leaving. This was a tumultuous period in American life. It began with the assassination of Martin Luther King, saw more and more opposition to the war in Vietnam, and ended with the election of Richard Nixon. Catholicism experienced a watershed event, the promulgation of *Humanae Vitae*, an encyclical banning the use of birth control. At the border, the church seemed to be an inkblot. When I asked, "Who is the Catholic church?" 60 percent of the Outs said it was the hierarchy or clergy; only 8 percent of the Ins did. To them the church was simply "the people." No matter how I asked the question, and I did many times in many ways, the contrast was immediate. One church here, another just across the line. And this despite identical—and intense—exposure to it.

The church that the Ins were in, in other words, was not the church that the Outs were out of. I am reminded of this at every skirmish in today's God wars. When neo-atheists use the word "religion," they evoke an image of fundamentalist Christianity that is inimical to science and "poisons everything." When theists use the word, they see a range of faiths mostly tolerant of science and even arising from same basic impulse. To them "religion" has flaws, but in the main it's a force for good. Here as well the contrast is stark: the religion the theists are in is not the religion the atheists are out of.

In my study of young adults, it became clear that positions on either side of the border were not reached on the basis of evidence, for the same evidence was acknowledged by both groups. Both mentioned unacceptable or irrelevant doctrines, racism among Catholics, the formalism and pomp of the hierarchy. The Outs, identifying these characteristics with the Catholic church, no longer wished to be a part of it. The Ins, considering the defects *one aspect* of the church, wished to remain members and even effect change. The "evidence," then, could be construed in a number of ways. Which way it *was* construed seemed more a question of wanting than a question of seeing. It had that a-rational starting-point.

And so I looked to beginnings. Ins, I found, were much more likely than Outs to have come from homes in which (1) both parents practiced Catholicism and (2) there were no gross disturbances such as divorce, separation, abandonment or alcoholism. These were "securely Catholic" homes, and in them a third factor was at work. Growing up, Ins felt closer than average to the parent of the same sex and Outs to the parent of the opposite sex. All three factors are the kind that lead to a deep internalization of parental values—in this case, the value of being Catholic. This value had little to do with reason, but it had a profound impact on reason later on. It had a profound effect on *seeing*.

Were corresponding factors at work in "securely atheistic" homes, I would expect a corresponding outcome—that children from these homes would maintain a secular worldview in adulthood, selecting evidence as Catholic Ins and Outs did. But that hypothesis awaits testing.

We should remember that the oldest person in my study was thirty-one, and that the influence of parents may diminish over time.

Unforeseen life events may take center stage. When Charles Darwin boarded the Beagle at the age of twenty-two, he was a firm believer in Genesis and had in fact completed studies for the ministry. Later in life he became what most describe as an agnostic. He abandoned religion not because of any evidence he found on the Galapagos nor because religion was incompatible with his theory of evolution. Though he had given up a belief in creationism, Darwin left religion only when his beloved daughter Annie fell ill and died. He could not reconcile that loss with Christianity's claim that a good and loving God cares about every hair on our heads.

As director of the Human Genome Project, Francis Collins led a scientific journey comparable to Darwin's. Yet his religious journey was nearly the opposite. At age of twenty-two Collins was an atheist, the son of freethinkers. He entered medical school and a few years later began having bedside conversations with sick and dying patients. Many were deeply religious and, despite their terrible suffering, they were at peace. "Suddenly all my arguments [for atheism] seemed very thin," Collins wrote in *The Language of God*. "I had the sensation that the ice under my feet was cracking." He began an intellectual search that led to C.S. Lewis and ultimately to Christianity, where his faith survived a trauma, though not a death, involving his daughter. This was a journey of reason, science, evidence and . . . bedside conversations. A *whole* life experience, a *whole* person making decisions about religion.

Biographies such as these are needed to complement studies like *The View from the Border*. In different ways, Charles Darwin and Francis Collins tell us what these Catholic Ins and Outs did, that catch-all metaphors like "spells" and "poison" are useless when describing religious experience on either side of a border. Only when we search for the ambiguities, the ironies and the paradoxes in the lives of both theists and atheists will we begin to comprehend the varieties of religious experience, as William James sought to do a century ago.

I would like to thank Irving Louis Horowitz, Transaction Publishers, and Google Book Search for making *The View from the Border* available once again. They couldn't have picked a better moment. And when that moment passes, it is good to know that this and countless other books will be ready for whatever comes, just a click or two away. It's a whole new world.

John Kotre

It is a classic principle of psychology that only against vague and ambiguous stimuli do people define themselves. In saying what one sees in a dream, an ink blot, an expressionless face, or a point of light, it seems that one says more about what is in and around him than what is in the stimulus.

PART I

Prelude

ONE

Why the Border

I began planning this study late in 1967 because I was curious about the periphery surrounding the Catholic Church. By "periphery" I had in mind the borderline existing between young people, raised as Catholics, who felt they had left the Church, and other young people, raised as Catholics, who still considered themselves within the bounds of the Church. The periphery seemed an ideal place to position myself for a social-psychological investigation for several reasons.

First, the border between being in and being out of the Church was becoming increasingly blurred. Twenty years before, one could feel safe in saying that those *in* the Catholic Church believed X, Y, and Z, and that those who had *left* the Church rejected X, Y, and Z. But there was becoming visible a growing number of young Catholics who either rejected or found irrelevant the bulk of Catholic dogma, who practiced their religion only sporadically, and yet who felt strong ties to the Church and clearly wanted to be a part of it. How were they different from those who, equally rejecting of Catholic dogma, had crossed the border and now saw themselves outside the Church?

The line of demarcation, if there was one, was quite ill-defined. Yet that line seemed to involve young adult Catholics at rather deep levels of their personality. Being raised a "good Catholic" in the United States meant that one received sixteen full years of Catholic education. One does not go through such a program without becoming deeply influenced by it, and when one reaches the point at which he examines where he has been, he is often plummeted into a profound intellectual-emotional crisis. The result of the crisis may be leaving the Church, or it may, on the other hand, be redefining what membership in the Church means. People at the border, perceiving the line as the vague, arbitrary thing it is, yet deeply involved in whatever it is: such a situation, I thought, should bring otherwise hidden psychological processes to the surface.

The periphery, secondly, was a place where change was occurring. I remembered a maxim attributed to Kurt Lewin that, if you want to understand anything, observe it as it changes, and I recalled that Emile Durkheim had said that the sacred element in society is the most resistant to change. A major religion in the process of change was a most significant situation, and one, again, in which latent psychological and sociological processes should be forced to the surface. Standing at the periphery I would be able to watch individuals in the process of change, and I could as well get a grass-roots perspective on a major institution in change.

My plan of attack was to interview one hundred graduates of Catholic colleges who were then graduate students at the University of Chicago or Northwestern University. Fifty of these students would consider themselves in the Catholic Church and fifty would consider themselves out, twenty-five males and twenty-five females in each category. I would also try to match Ins and Outs on other variables such as graduate school attended and field of study.

I developed a structured questionnaire to cover each subject's present beliefs, values, perceptions of the Catholic

Church, perceptions of his parents, and, of course, the reasons why he considered himself in or out of the Church. The questionnaire, which I was to administer to each subject individually, turned out to be forty-four pages long for Ins and forty pages long for Outs (see Appendix II).

Interviewing people on both sides of the border would enable me, I assumed, to do a number of things:

(1) to document the change taking place in the Catholic Church. Most specifically, this would mean finding out what young Catholics actually did believe, value, and think of the Church. It would mean finding out precisely what was and what was not left of a borderline in 1968. Was belief in a Trinity, or in papal infallibility, or in man's free will what distinguished Ins and Outs? Or was the criterion one of religious practice? Might there be differing values regarding social or political life, regarding the desirability of intellectual pursuits, and so on? If a religion in the process of change is a significant event, it appeared wise to document that event as it happened.

(2) to bring to the borderline a number of theoretical questions from social psychology. The subjects I would interview seemed ideal for testing theoretical statements about decision making, information seeking, tolerance for ambiguity, and cognitive consistency, topics generally included under the rubric "attitude change." Hypotheses from personality theory and even from sociological theories of organizations, it appeared, could be investigated with profit at the border.

On April 2, 1968, two days before the first of two assassinations that occupied the nation's consciousness, and a week before President Johnson's announcement of a bombing pause in North Vietnam, I interviewed my first subject. On December 4, a month after Richard Nixon had been elected president, I interviewed my last. Much had occurred in the eight months that intervened: the Democratic convention in Chicago, the presidential campaign itself, and, more directly related to this study, the pope's encyclical on contraception. One major change in the subject selection procedure had to be made (see Chapter 2). A follow-up questionnaire was also mailed in November to those subjects interviewed prior to the pope's encyclical to see whether his ban on contraception had any effect on their belief system.

More significant than changes in plans for executing the investigation, however, were changes in me, in my conception of what I was doing and of how I would organize my data. As the eight months of interviewing wore on, I began to realize that people who were exposed to similar kinds of information about the Catholic Church were describing it in quite dissimilar ways. I began to think of the Catholic Church as a macrocosmic ink blot, a completely ambiguous stimulus, like the stationary dot of light that, in a totally darkened room, appears to move in an irregular fashion. Why this dot of light, the Catholic Church, appeared to some people to move in one direction and to others to move in an opposite direction, when they know similar things about it, became the question that dominated my thinking. I felt the reasons lay more in the people themselves than in the Catholic Church.

Broadening my perspective, I became aware that it was not the Catholic Church but religion in general that was so ambiguous. If one shares in enough experiences of the religious impulse, he is left with the conclusion that God is the most arbitrary of stimuli. He may either be a projection of our own needs and desires, our own reflection in the water, or indeed a transcendent being existing over and apart from us. In describing one's God, if he has one, one becomes eminently aware that he is describing himself.

I also came to realize that my concern with the border around Catholicism meant that I was a product of my times, that many people at this point in history are walking any number of borders, juggling relationships with communities to which they, willingly or not, belong. For blacks, there are positions to be taken at the interface between their own ethnic community and larger white society, and there are appropriate designations for those who appear too borderline, too marginal. Indians, facing white society, are, in the words of a recent TV documentary, "between two rivers." The young who face the draft are often figuratively and literally on the border of the United States. Workers move between two jobs; professors have joint appointments; and each can moonlight—but only if another border, that between work and family, does not become a source of conflict. People sit on fences, walk tightropes, wear two hats, steer middle courses, take the best of both worlds, become marginal to one community so as to be central to another, become deviant in one so as to accept the norms of another. At other times, they simply cross the border, abandoning one group and its set of norms for another.

Why so many people are at so many borders at this time may not be difficult to ascertain. Communities, including formal institutions, are changing at a pace more rapid than before. New ones are being born; others are splitting; and still others are dying. In the process, the meaning of membership in each becomes blurred and individuals are sent scurrying from one position to another. Individuals, too, are exposed through the mass media to a pluralism of communities they were unaware of before and so come to realize the parochialism of their own. And people are more mobile than ever. The suitcases are never fully unpacked as old jobs and residences are left for new ones.

Those communities that are entered and left—or partly entered and partly left—are often in some degree antagonistic to each other, and the individual who moves from one to the other, or lives for a time between both, is caught between conflicting forces. Communities that change likewise catch individuals in the middle and force them to take whatever positions in the resulting ambiguity that fit their needs. Why, as communities change, as they are entered and left, border walkers take the positions they do, I saw as the larger scope of this inquiry.

As to those social-psychological propositions that I originally thought would be testable, I found they had little relevance at the borderline. Instead, new applications for psychological theory became apparent. The psychology of sex differences took on importance, as did developmental psychology, especially as it focused on parent-child relations. I also recognized that what I was tapping could be tapped equally well in the study of other belief systems or world views. I began to call what I was doing a psychology of "what's it all about," something having to do with viewing ambiguity and positioning oneself amidst it. As such, the work paralleled what had already been done in greater depth in studies of attitudes toward Russia and perceptions of that most ambiguous of stimuli, the nation's enemy.

I should note, finally, that I was part of the process I observed, that as I studied these one hundred people, I was inevitably studying myself. I was a border walker, more in than out of the Church, with the same Catholic upbringing, encountering the same society, as these subjects. Had I not been, the study would have gone undone, or at least its most important questions would have gone unasked. I had found the working material for psychological investigation in my own back yard and decided to take advantage of it.

A number of classic psychological forays have followed the same pattern. Freud drew as much from himself as from his patients in constructing psychoanalysis, and Piaget based much of his theory of early cognitive development on detailed observations of his own three children. More recently, studies of prejudice and accounts of life in the ghetto have been written by those who have felt the effects of prejudice or have been confined within the ghetto's walls.

The danger in such an approach is that the investigator may be especially subject to biases in interpreting the data he collects. I have tried, naturally, to avoid these biases and have presented the data as completely as possible so that someone else, if he is so inclined, can suggest alternate explanations. When collecting the data itself, I took the precautions described in Chapter 2 so that my position with respect to the Church would have little effect on the respondent.

What follows is the information gathered from these one hundred subjects and an explanation of the major differences between those who define themselves as Ins and those who define themselves as Outs. Chapter 2 tells how the subjects were located, what the general background information on them was, and takes up the question of biasing interviewer effects. Chapter 3 contains brief case histories of selected Ins and Outs and so gives an idea in real life terms of the thinking and events that led to their present status. "The Results of Change" sets forth what the subjects currently believe (Chapter 4), what they value and how these values relate to the Church (Chapter 5), and how they perceive the Catholic Church (Chapter 6). As "The Search for Why" is begun, sex is related to In-Out status, accounts of change, beliefs, values, and perceptions of the Church (Chapter 7); associations between one's In or Out status and his description of his parents are examined in detail (Chapter 8); and an overall explanation of major In-Out differences is presented (Chapter 9). Finally, under "Extensions" I use data to speculate about the future of the present subjects and about the permeability of the Church as an institution (Chapters 10 and 11).

TWO

One Hundred Young Adults: Who They Were and Where They Started

Prior to presenting the results of this investigation, we must describe the people involved: who they were, where they came from, how I happened to contact them, and what they understood about me. Since this study involves attitude change, it is also important to ascertain, as well as possible from retrospective data, the extent to which subjects in each of the two major groups (Ins and Outs) *started at the same point* with respect to Catholicism. We will begin, therefore, by discussing (1) how the subjects were located and how they assigned themselves to either of the two major groups, (2) possible interviewer effects in collecting the data, (3) the demographic information on the subjects, and (4) how salient Catholicism had been to them before they began to re-evaluate it.

Locating the Subjects

The sources from which the subjects in each major group were obtained are listed in Table 2.1. The first subjects were

Ins who came from volunteer lists posted at Calvert House, a Catholic student center on the University of Chicago campus, and Sheil Chapel, a similar center at Northwestern. The remaining eighty subjects were located through these initial subjects, through later subjects, and through other means mentioned in Table 2.1. Ins were the usual source of other Ins, and Outs of other Outs.

Table 2.1. Source of Subjects

	Ins (N)	Outs (N)
Volunteered through Catholic centers on campus	19	1
Name suggested by previous In subject	17	10
Name suggested by previous Out subject	7	27
Other	7	12
Total	50	50

Note: $\chi^2 = 31.10$, $df = 3$, $p < .001$. "Other" includes names suggested by nonsubjects and volunteers responding to ads in school papers and notices in Church bulletins.

At the end of the one-and-a-half to two hour interview, I generally asked the subject for the names of friends who might be willing to participate in the study. Those whom I called at the suggestion of previous subjects almost unanimously agreed to an interview. Some had to be passed up, however, because they failed to meet the requirements for being included in the subject pool (see Tables 2.3, 2.5, and 2.6). Only two out of the nearly one hundred I called flatly declined to be interviewed.

Since this study took as its starting point a person's own definition of whether he was in or out of the Church, it was critical in making a "pitch" for subjects not to force a definition upon them. Subjects knew before agreeing to be interviewed that this was a study of "the borderline between membership and ex-membership in the Catholic Church" and that "questions in the interview concern your present beliefs, values, perceptions of the Church, and reasons why you are still a member or no longer a member of the Church." They knew that one hundred graduates of Catholic colleges were needed, fifty Ins and fifty Outs, twenty-five males and twenty-five females in each category.

Most of the people included in the study were fairly clear about their status with respect to the Church even if they had given it little thought recently. If a person was basically ambiguous about his status, he was not interviewed, one of the criteria for subject selection being "they considered themselves either in the Church or out of the Church." Eight people (one male, seven females) with whom I spoke were not interviewed because they could not assign themselves to either category. They said, for example: "I don't put down 'Catholic,' but I'm not sure there isn't some sense in which I am still a member of the Catholic Church. I just couldn't say."[1] Or: "I don't know myself if I am in or out. I do not attend Church myself, but I do with my mother and family."

Subjects considering themselves *in* often expressed concern about *whose* definition of membership was to be taken, saying for example: "The official Church might not consider me in, but I do." Or: "I'm in but unorthodox. Ten years ago I would have been out."

The status of the above two people may not have been clear to an outsider, but it was clear to them, and so they were included as subjects. On several occasions, prospective subjects were suggested to me as Outs and turned out to consider themselves in. The reverse was also true: several prospective Ins told me they were out. One subject classified herself over the

---

1. This quotation and the five that follow are paraphrases of what I was told on the phone. Those quotations from subjects that appear in later chapters are taken from the interview protocols.

phone as an Out, only to say when I arrived to interview her that she was in. It had become clear to her in the interim that it was *her* criteria that mattered.

Some subjects felt ambiguity about their status, but nevertheless considered themselves *out* of the Church. The most borderline of these said, for example: "Well, if I had to choose, I would say I am out of the Church. People ask me what my status is, and I don't like to classify myself one way or the other; but, if you asked me, I'd say yes, I am out of the Church." Another said, "That depends on what criteria you use for being in or out. I go to Church on Sunday, but that is force of habit while I am in the state of flux; it does me no harm to do it. In terms of the basic values and norms of the Church, I am out. More basically, I am out."

A person's self-definition of status may seem an arbitrary criterion upon which to base the major division of subjects in this study. In some kinds of research, using such an arbitrary criterion could be justifiably questioned. But in the present study an arbitrary situation was *sought out*. Many subjects said they did not care whether they were in or out, or found such a dichotomy "irrelevant." Nevertheless, they had a fairly clear perception of their position on either side of the tenuous line between In and Out, and as a follow-up questionnaire indicates (Chapter 10), they continue to perceive themselves as they originally did. The question this study asks is: why is there such a perception in this seemingly irrelevant ambiguity? If strong associations are found between self-definitions and other variables, then the self-definitions cannot be as whimsical as it first appears.

Possible Interviewer Effects

A great deal of emphasis in behavioral research has been placed on "interviewer effects," i.e., an interviewer unconsciously communicating his biases and expectations to the subject he is interviewing (Hyman, 1954; Kahn and Cannell, 1957; Rosenthal, 1966). In the present study there was such a danger. For example, if a subject perceived me as an In Catholic, he might be more inclined to give orthodox answers to some of the questions and to express less hostility toward the Church. On the other hand, if he perceived me as an Out Catholic, he might lean toward less orthodox answers or express more dissatisfaction with the Church. For these reasons, it seemed advisable for me to remain as anonymous as possible.

I did this by excluding from the subject pool people who knew me personally and by telling subjects before the interview to "make no assumptions about my particular relation to Catholicism." Nor did I reveal my status once the interview was over since new subjects were to be located through those I had already interviewed. I did, however, ask the subjects what they thought my relation to Catholicism might be. Their estimates, made at the end of the interviews, are presented in Table 2.2.

Several conclusions can be drawn about the subjects' perception of me. (1) No clear-cut impression of my status was communicated to all subjects. Thirty-six per cent of the sub-

Table 2.2. Subjects' Estimation of the Interviewer's Relation to Catholicism

	Ins (N)	Outs (N)
Subjects estimating I was an *In* Catholic	22	16
Subjects estimating I was an *Out* Catholic or *Never* Catholic	5	9
Subjects estimating I was either an *In* Catholic or an *Out* Catholic (i.e., at least once Catholic), but unable to specify which	6	6
Subjects saying they could not estimate	17	19
Total	50	50

Note: In-out differences are not statistically significant ($p < .05$, χ^2 test).

jects could not make a guess as to what my status was despite the fact that the most logical guess would be that I was an In Catholic. (2) When an impression was given, it generally was that I was an In Catholic (38 per cent), though 14 per cent estimated I was not a Catholic. Saying that I was in seemed most reasonable because someone who was not a Catholic would not have the interest to pursue such a study and because only an insider would be able to ask the kinds of questions that were asked. (3) Different impressions were not given to Ins and Outs. There was a slight, but statistically insignificant tendency for Ins to see me as Catholic and Outs to see me as not Catholic. On occasion I must have reflected the orientation of the subject, though this did not happen enough to produce major differences in the two groups' perception of me.

While it appears that no biasing effects were produced by the interview, it cannot be said that the interview produced no change in the subjects. Indeed, it was on occasion a fairly significant event for them. One subject, for example, had the idea prior to the interview that I was a priest and that the interview would be her concrete way of saying she was out of the Church. Other subjects welcomed the interview as a way of sorting out their thoughts about the Church. It forced them into reflection they otherwise might not have undertaken and, no doubt, served to reinforce their definition of themselves as In or Out.

Demographic Information

I had the impression as I travelled from one end of Chicago to the other in pursuit of interviews that graduates of Catholic colleges had filtered into every possible niche of graduate school life. For those subjects who were not graduate students, a broad variety of life styles was evidenced. Representation along the political spectrum seemed complete, from subjects on the left who advocated an "American revolution" and were involved in radical political action to one on the right who disapproved of "encyclicals that imply the poor have a right to the possessions of the rich."

I conducted interviews at all hours of the day and night, most of them in apartments around the two campuses. Some interviews were carried on in Calvert House, some in older homes on the Northwest side, several in plush suburban homes and Gold Coast apartments. Others were conducted on the Midway Plaisance and on benches overlooking Lake Michigan. I drank wine, beer, 7-Up, and Pepsi, ate sandwiches, cookies, and ice cream, was crawled on by cats, snapped at by dogs, and burped on by babies. Signs on apartment walls announced, "There are no great poets without great audiences," "Commitment brings fulfillment," and "Souffrir passe, avoir souffert ne passe jamais." Background sounds included the chant of Gethsemane monks, Richard Nixon's last minute campaign appeal, and a group welcoming the return of a member of the olive underground. Clearly, the interviewees were not of a type.

It becomes necessary, then, to look carefully at the demographic information on the subjects to see if there is the same degree of variety among Ins and Outs. The differences that do appear must be kept in mind as possible explanations of the subjects' desire to remain in or leave the Church.

Most of the characteristics listed in Table 2.3 show no differences between Ins and Outs. Since subjects had to be native-born United States citizens between the ages of twenty-

Table 2.3. General Demographic Information on Subjects

	Ins (N)	Outs (N)
Native-born United States citizen[a]	50	50
Sex[a]		
(1) Male	25	25
(2) Female	25	25
Age[a] Mean	24.26	24.14
Range	21-31	22-29

Table 2.3.—Continued

	Ins (N)	Outs (N)
Marital status		
(1) Single	11	30
(2) Married	39	20
Number of children[b] Mean	1.64 (N=11)	0.75 (N=20)
Range	0-4	0-3
Own income (family income, if married)[c]		
(1) Under $5,000	34	21
(2) $5,000 to $7,500	7	18
(3) $7,501 to $10,000	6	7
(4) Over $10,000	3	4
Place of birth[d]		
(1) Northeastern U.S.	17	10
(2) North Central U.S.	23	31
(3) Southern and Western U.S.	7	4
(4) Undetermined	3	5
Ethnic background[e]		
(1) Irish	19	18
(2) German	11	13
(3) Polish	5	2
(4) Italian	4	3
(5) French	1	1
(6) English	2	3
(7) Spanish	2	0
(8) East European	3	7
(9) Other, or no predominant nationality	3	3
Mother born in U.S.		
(1) Yes	48	47
(2) No	2	3
Mother's education		
(0) Did not complete grammar school	0	1
(1) Graduate of grammar school	8	6
(2) Graduate of high school	28	27
(3) Graduate of college	12	12
(4) Has M.A.	2	4
Mother's occupation		
(1) Housewife	33	28
(2) Housewife and part time employment	9	8
(3) Housewife and full time employment	8	14

Table 2.3.—Continued

	Ins (N)	Outs (N)
Father born in U.S.[f]		
(1) Yes	46	45
(2) No	4	4
Father's education		
(0) Did not complete grammar school	2	1
(1) Graduate of grammar school	7	9
(2) Graduate of high school	22	20
(3) Graduate of college	11	9
(4) Has M.A.	2	3
(5) Has professional degree	6	5
(6) Has Ph.D.	0	2
Father's occupation		
(1) Blue-collar	15	13
(2) White-collar	29	28
(3) Professional	6	6
Parents' income (at time S was 15 years of age)		
(1) Under $5,000	1	4
(2) $5,000 to $10,000	25	22
(3) $10,001 to $15,000	11	14
(4) $15,001 to $20,000	5	4
(5) Over $20,000	8	5
Number of siblings Mean	2.88	2.94
Range	0-11	0-11

Note: Unless specifically footnoted, In-Out differences on each variable are not statistically significant ($p < .05$, χ^2 or t test).

[a]It was required that subjects be native-born U.S. citizens between the ages of 21 and 31. There were to be 25 males and 25 females in each major category. Five subjects interviewed were not included in the one hundred because they failed to meet these requirements.

[b]$t = 2.24$, $p < .05$, 2-tailed.

[c]$\chi^2 = 8.13$, $df = 3$, $p < .05$.

[d]See Table 2.4 for classification of the states.

[e]Predominant nationality or, if two nationalities equal, the father's nationality.

[f]Several of the variables involving the father do not total 100 because the father was deceased or absent from the home.

one and thirty-one to be included in the study, and since there were to be twenty-five males and twenty-five females in each major category, Ins and Outs are matched in these characteristics. They are also well matched in terms of ethnic background, parents' education, parents' occupation, parents' income, number of siblings, and they are not significantly different in birthplace or marital status.

The Ins that were married, however, had more children than the married Outs, but this difference in family size is not large enough, nor does it involve enough subjects to be of serious concern. Outs had a slightly higher income level than Ins. The Outs' higher income level is due to the major demographic difference to be discussed below: a number of female Outs were not or had not been in graduate school at the time of the interview and either worked full time or were married to husbands who worked full time.

The college backgrounds of subjects are also well equated (Table 2.4). The one hundred subjects came from forty-three colleges across the United States, Ins representing a greater variety of colleges (32) than Outs (21). More Outs were from colleges in the north central United States, this due again to the presence of nongraduate-school female Outs who tended to come from local schools. The most frequently represented college was Loyola University of Chicago (23 subjects).

I hoped, and so it turned out, that the college backgrounds of Ins and Outs would be similar, because being in or out might otherwise be related to differing educational experiences. Table 2.4 shows that Marquette University is the only school with a significant overrepresentation among one of the groups. Five Outs attended Marquette full time and one part time. No Ins from Marquette were interviewed. This should not be taken to mean that Marquette produces only Outs, however, because I had the names of at least three prospective Ins from Marquette. They were not interviewed because the quota of one hundred was filled before they were contacted.

Table 2.4. Undergraduate Catholic Colleges Attended by Subjects

	Ins	Outs	Both Ins and Outs
Number of *different* colleges attended	32 Colleges	21 Colleges	43 Colleges

	Ins (N)	Outs (N)
Principle colleges attended[a]		
(1) Loyola University (Chicago)	9	12.5[b]
(2) University of Notre Dame	4	2
(3) Marquette University	0	5.5[c]
(4) Saint Xavier College (Chicago)	2	3
(5) Emmanuel College (Boston)	3	2
(6) Boston College	1	3
(7) College of the Holy Cross	1	3

	Ins (N)	Outs (N)
Location of colleges attended[d]		
(1) Northeastern U.S.	15	13
(2) North Central U.S.	26	35
(3) Southern and Western U.S.	9	2
Total	50	50

[a]Listed if four or more subjects were from the college.
[b]Several subjects spent only half their college years at the college listed.
[c]Marquette is the only college with a significantly uneven representation among Ins and Outs (binomial test $p < .05$, 2-tailed). See the text, however.
[d]Northeastern states: Connecticut, Maine, Massachusetts, New Hampshire, New Jersey, New York, Pennsylvania, Rhode Island, Vermont. North central states: Illinois, Indiana, Iowa, Kansas, Michigan, Minnesota, Missouri, Nebraska, North Dakota, Ohio, South Dakota, Wisconsin. Southern and western states: all others. A chi-square test comparing the location of colleges attended by Ins and Outs yields $\chi^2 = 5.93$, $df = 2$, $.06 > p > .05$.

That there is a balance between the colleges attended by Ins and those attended by Outs does not mean the college environment is not important in determining one's position with respect to the Church. What it does mean is that *in this study* being in or out of the Catholic Church cannot be related to one's college environment. We can assume that the fifty Ins and fifty Outs of this study were exposed to quite similar information environments in college. They may have perceived those environments in different ways—and indeed they did— just as presently they perceive the Catholic Church in different ways. The reasons for the differing perceptions of *these* one hundred people, however, cannot be found in the colleges they attended, for college background turns out to have been held constant.

The major difference between Ins and Outs is in the graduate school status of subjects (Table 2.5), and this difference is the result of a change in plans for finding interviewees. Originally, plans were for a 2 × 2 × 2 design (Status: In-Out; Sex: Male-Female; Graduate school: Chicago-Northwestern) with twelve to thirteen subjects in each of the eight cells. For male subjects, recruitment went according to plan. It was extremely difficult, however, to locate female Outs who were graduate students. After more than five months of searching, only two had been found. The decision was made, therefore, to widen the sampling area for female Out subjects. No longer did they have to be graduate students at Northwestern or Chicago; they simply had to be graduates of a Catholic college. Preferably they would be attending or would have attended some graduate school or be part of a graduate school community (e.g., the wife of a graduate student), but this would not be an essential requirement. By widening the sampling area, twenty-five female Outs were located before the study dragged on indefinitely.

It was also decided to accept some female Ins from this wider sampling area. The female In group would be a compromise group between male Ins and female Outs, i.e., it would have enough graduate students in it to make meaningful comparisons with male Ins, but it would also have enough nongraduate students to enable meaningful comparisons with female Outs. This part of the plan was only partially successful. (See Table 2.5 for the graduate school status of all subjects.)

Table 2.5. Graduate School Status of Subjects at Time of Interview

	Males		Females[a]	
	Ins (N)	Outs (N)	Ins (N)	Outs (N)
(1) Graduate student at Northwestern University	13	13	7	2
(2) Graduate student at the University of Chicago	12	12	11	1
(3) Graduate student elsewhere			2	1
(4) Former graduate student with advanced degree			2	2
(5) Former graduate student without advanced degree			1	6
(6) Never attended graduate school			2	13
Total	25	25	25	25

Graduate school field (for subjects in categories 1-4 above)[b]	Ins (N)	Outs (N)
(1) Law and medicine	4	6
(2) Social work	5	1
(3) Education	3	1
(4) Journalism, business, library science	6	1
(5) Physical and biological science	5	0
(6) Social science	8	5
(7) Humanities	9	15
(8) Religion	6	1
(9) Other	1	1
Total	47	31
Year in graduate school (for subjects in categories 1-3 above)[c] Mean	2.04 (N=45)	2.41 (N=29)
Range	1–6	1–6

Note: "Graduate student" includes law and medical students; all graduate students were full time unless in the final stages of obtaining a degree.

[a]A 3 × 2 chi-square test comparing graduate school status of female Ins and female Outs (Categories: Presently, Formerly, or Never graduate student) yields $\chi^2 = 21.01$, $df = 2$, $p < .005$.

[b]In-Out differences in each field are not statistically significant ($p < .05$, binomial test, 2-tailed).

[c]In-Out difference is not statistically significant ($p < .05$, t test, 2-tailed).

The problem of not finding female Outs in graduate school could have meant that the method of locating subjects was not suited to female Outs, perhaps because they were not as public about their status as males. There is stronger evidence, though, that fewer female Outs were in the given sampling area, that females were simply less likely than males to define themselves as out of the Catholic Church (see Chapter 7).

Because of the change in sampling procedure, it will be necessary, before drawing any conclusions about sex differences, to see whether graduate-school female Outs responded differently to questionnaire items than did nongraduate-school female Outs. Otherwise, differences due in fact to graduate school status may be misinterpreted as due to sex.

Those Ins and Outs in graduate school are nearly balanced as far as length of time in graduate school is concerned. Outs, however, are slightly overrepresented in the humanities (philosophy, history, language, literature), while Ins are overrepresented in social work, journalism and other practical fields, as well as in the physical and biological sciences and religion. None of these differences, however, is statistically significant.

There are, in summary, a substantial number of areas in which the fifty Ins match the fifty Outs. There are a few in which they do not match, the most important being graduate school status. Thirteen female Outs, as compared with two female Ins, had never been in graduate school.

All one hundred of these subjects are clearly not representative of American Catholicism at large, as can be seen from a 1963–64 national survey of American Catholics (Greeley and Rossi, 1966). Respondents in that survey were limited to adults between the ages of twenty-three and fifty-seven, with only one-sixth of the total falling between twenty-three and twenty-nine, the category closest to ours. Of all respondents, under 3 per cent had sixteen full years of Catholic education. If these respondents are equally distributed across the various age categories, we can make the rough estimate that the age and college background of our subjects is representative of some fraction of 1 per cent of adult American Catholics. When we add the consideration that most of our subjects are currently attending graduate school, their representativeness of adult American Catholics decreases even further.

A sense of the discrepancy between the present subjects and adult American Catholicism is conveyed by a finding from a July, 1968, probability survey of Catholics aged sixteen and over in the diocese of Worcester, Massachusetts, a diocese covering an area heavily Catholic (57 per cent), one whose bishop is described as actively implementing Vatican II, and one whose general population profile is close to that of the United States at large. Of those Catholics interviewed in this survey, 43 per cent said they had never heard of an event called the Second Vatican Council (Becker Research Corp., 1969).

The present subjects, then, are not representative of adult American Catholics because they have had more socialization into Catholicism than others, because they are among the best products of the Catholic educational system (having been accepted at graduate institutions of high academic rating), and because they are younger than others. In short, they represent the best that Catholicism turns out, and, as such, should be considered a sensitive barometer to the pressures that exist within the Church.

Original Salience of Catholicism

Differences in the belief systems, value systems, and feelings of Ins and Outs regarding the Church can be considered a product of change only if it can be shown that Ins and Outs were *once alike* in their attitudes toward Catholicism. It would have been desirable, of course, to interview these subjects both before and after change occurred, but since that was impossible, the next best thing was to ask them to reflect on their early feeling toward and practice of Catholicism.

At the outset of each interview, the subject was asked, "How important was it to you to be a Catholic at various times in your life?" He then rated the importance (in the sense of valuing Catholicism positively) at four times in his life: eighth grade, senior year of high school, senior year of college, and presently. The mean ratings of Ins and Outs are presented in Figure 2.1.

Outs describe Catholicism as being slightly more important to them in eighth grade than do Ins; perhaps it appears so important now in contrast to their present feelings. The ratings for their senior year high school are the same; a split appears by their senior year of college and is wider at the present time. Personal reflection, then, shows the Outs at least as positive as Ins in their early feelings toward Catholicism.

More substantial indices of the early importance of Catholicism are presented in Table 2.6. There is little or no difference in the amount of Catholic education received by In and Out subjects, most of them having had a full sixteen years. Their attendance at Mass was also quite similar, almost none having omitted Sunday Mass for any period of time, and about half in each group having attended daily Mass for a period of time. There were a few more ex-seminarians and ex-religious among Ins (nine) than Outs (three), but the difference is not statistically significant. The two groups appear, then, to have been quite close in their early attitudes toward the Church.

Summary

One hundred recent graduates of Catholic colleges, fifty who considered themselves in the Catholic Church and fifty who said they had left it, were contacted through informal means and given an interview of one-and-a-half to two hours.

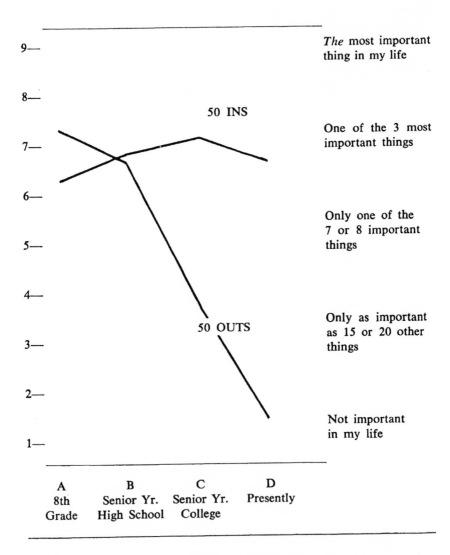

Figure 2.1. Subjects' ratings (expressed in mean scores) of "How important was it to you to be a Catholic at various times in your life?" The In-Out difference between ratings is significant at times A (t = 2.87, p < .01, 2-tailed), C (t = 7.77, p < .001, 2-tailed), and D (t = 18.68, p < .001, 2-tailed); the difference is not significant at time B.

Table 2.6. Indices of The Salience of Catholicism Prior to Subjects' Re-evaluation of It

	Ins (N)	Outs (N)
Born Catholic		
(1) Yes	49	50
(2) No	1	0
Attended Catholic grammar school		
(1) Yes	42	39
(2) Part time	3	6
(3) No	5	5
Attended Catholic high school		
(1) Yes	42	41
(2) Part time	1	1
(3) No	7	8
Attended Catholic college[a]		
(1) Yes	48	48
(2) Part time	2	2
(3) No	0	0
Ever omitted Sunday Mass for a period of time (prior to re-evaluation)		
(1) Yes	0	3
(2) No	50	47
Ever attended daily Mass voluntarily		
(1) at least 5 extra times per week for one school year		
Yes	26	24
No	24	26
(2) at least 2 extra times per week for 5 years		
Yes	28	25
No	22	25
(3) never a period of extra voluntary attendance		
Yes	3	6
No	47	44
Ever studied to be a priest or religious[b]		
(1) Yes	9	3
(2) No	41	47

Note: None of the In-Out differences above is statistically significant ($p < .05$, χ^2 test).

[a]Attendance at and graduation from a Catholic college was a requirement for subjects. "Part time college" means: S spent first year college at non-Catholic school (1 In); S spent third year college in Europe (1 In, 1 Out); S 12 hours short of graduation (1 Out).

[b]No subject was *currently* studying to be a priest or religious.

These Ins and Outs did not differ significantly in their perception of me (the interviewer), and they were closely matched on a number of demographic characteristics as well. The major characteristic on which they were not equated was graduate school status: most subjects were graduate students at Northwestern University or the University of Chicago, but a disproportionate number of female Outs were not. Judging from their recollections of the past importance of Catholicism and their report of past religious practice, these fifty Ins and fifty Outs were once a relatively homogeneous group of one hundred Ins, and what is described in Chapter 3 can be accurately called change.

THREE

The Period of Change

One hundred people, apparently alike in their Catholic upbringing, enrolled at forty-three different Catholic colleges
sometime in the late fifties and early sixties. At some point in
the next four years, most of them entered a critical period of
evaluating their own Catholic background and beliefs. In the
end, fifty dissociated themselves from the Catholic Church and
fifty did not. In order to understand why these positions were
reached, it is necessary to describe in detail certain events
that led individuals on the road to change.

The change did begin, generally, in college. Before the data
was collected, I thought the catalyst of change might be the
transition from a Catholic college to a non-Catholic graduate
school where, for the first time, information discrepant with
one's Catholic beliefs would be encountered. Sixty subjects,
however, said the process of change began during attendance
at a Catholic college, and only twenty-six reported it began
after college (ten said it had begun before college, and four—
female Ins—felt there had been no real change). That the
change was initiated in college means either or both (1) that
Catholic colleges are not as intellectually isolated as one might
think (discrepant information was being encountered there)

29

and (2) that there is a certain point in late adolescence at which questioning of one's past takes place regardless of the environment.

While it was very difficult for subjects to pinpoint when the change began and when it ended, the average length of time between beginning and end was one to two years. Typically, the process began during college and gradually terminated only after college. Only twenty-eight said the crisis was settled before graduation. Thirty-one (twenty-nine Ins) said the change was still going on: generally, they did not expect it to end, though the anxiety level was down and their status probably would not change. Four subjects reported there had been no substantial change.

The re-evaluation did involve a good deal of crisis. Asked of their change, "How much of a crisis was involved in all this? By 'crisis' I mean the feeling of indecision, anxiety, pressure, and so on,"[1] subjects replied with such phrases as:

> a major turbulence over senior year
>
> remarkably little
>
> very much crisis—traumatic for the first months
>
> as much as could be—I was completely alone and it involved the commitment of my whole life
>
> no sleepless nights—more wonder than pressure or upset
>
> to the point of psychological counseling—intense pressure
>
> The dominant emotion was rage—trying to kick the Church in the ass to be what it should be. Then I said it's not worth it.

1. See Appendix II, p. 208, Question 5.

very little—more joy than a crisis

was so easy my wife said I was faking it

some, but always in the back of my mind was the thought I would never make it out

very severe—felt I was losing hope

very little conscious pressure, but the conflict lingers on

great emotional and psychological turmoil

Fifty-two subjects regarded the crisis as moderate or severe. Thirty-five thought it slight, and nine felt there was no crisis involved in the change. Asked to categorize their change in a different way, nineteen said the crisis was either the biggest or one of the two biggest in their lives, and fifty-two recalled it as at least one of the three biggest. Averaging for all subjects, the crisis was roughly one of the five or six biggest in their lives.

The individual experiences of change were quite diverse, no pattern of re-evaluation appearing that was common to more than three or four subjects. In view of this diversity, perhaps the best way to describe what happened is to present some brief individual accounts of change and then those few generalizations that can be made about all the subjects in a particular category. The short narratives that follow were selected on the basis of their representativeness and the amount of detail they manifested.

Ten Ins

Senior year in a southern college marked the beginning of some serious reflection for S.D. He had married a Catholic as an undergraduate and was already the father of one. Looking forward to a career in science, but tied down by responsibility for his wife and child, he found himself asking difficult questions about his family, his career, and his personal life. The questioning necessarily spilled over into his religion.

He came to Chicago as a research technician and there, over a number of years, had three more children, acquired an M.A., rose to the position of senior investigator and, at the age of twenty-eight, enrolled in a Ph.D. program. Shortly after coming to Chicago, too, he found that his reflections on Catholicism, which began simply as "questioning more deeply the things I had taken for granted," had become an intellectual crisis that involved "tremendous anxiety." He struggled with beliefs about God, the Trinity, the Resurrection, and evolution. He read voraciously, the best writer, he said, being Teilhard de Chardin. He kept in touch with a priest who respected him and found his experience enlightening. Through it all, however, he found that he could not get away from the Church, and at the end he became convinced of several ideas "to the degree that anyone can be convinced."

First, he became assured of the idea of God, and then, something much more difficult, of the idea of Christ. Since the Catholic Church, he reasoned, had the true link with Christ, he would remain a Catholic, this despite his inability to accept the notion of sin and confession and his feeling that the Church was dragging its feet in the area of social justice. Above all, the Church had the Eucharist. "The Eucharist keeps me a Catholic." If the Church ever changed its view relative to the Eucharist, S.D. said, he would be plunged into crisis once again.

Discontent and change seemed imminent for L.B. when he kept encountering opposition from his bishop while working as a Christian Brother in an inner-city poverty area. Questions about what he did and did not believe already had begun simmering, and this confrontation with the bishop brought these questions closer to the surface. The most significant outcome of his thinking, which never reached critical proportions, was leaving the Brothers. Their way of life was too authoritarian, and they were moving into the suburbs rather than concentrating on the inner city.

His present feelings about being in or out of the Church are not strong. He simply will consider himself in until there is some definite decision to leave (which there probably won't be) or until the Church "stops its development, redefines itself in terms of authoritarian categories and claims it is the sole avenue to salvation." While not a regular attender at Sunday Mass, he finds some validity in the liturgy and sacramental life of the Church. He cannot, however, accept the pomp and circumstance and general affluence of Church authorities. He regards the Church's formalism and legalism as equally distasteful, but thinks these are changing. The doctrines of the Assumption, of papal infallibility and "the magical interpretation of just about everything" are unattractive, but he can interpret them in an acceptable way. A divinity student, he recognizes that membership in various churches is determined only by an accident of birth, and he reacts against being denominationalized as a Catholic.

Being Catholic to A.N. means little more than being Christian or simply being religious. As an undergraduate he began reading Protestant theologians and underwent "not a revolution, but an expansion." He never thought about abandoning the Catholic Church or Christianity—he never could have become Protestant instead of Catholic—but he could and did become both by "adding a Protestant dimension to my Christianity." Protestantism's attractiveness lay in its development of individualism; the appeal of Catholicism was its emphasis on community, sacramentalism, mystery and ritual.

The anxiety involved in his expansion derived from his divorce from the firm strictures of Catholicism such as going to confession (he doesn't), attending Sunday Mass (he goes once a month), and abstaining from meat on Friday. A small crisis developed when he refused to sign a statement prior to marriage promising to follow the teachings of the Church on birth control. Eventually he did sign, defining "Church" for himself as all the people in the Church, not just the magisterium.

He wishes to be a Christian because the sense of transcendence and sacramentalism is meaningful to him and because he believes in Christ as a religious answer to anxiety and suffering. He regards himself as a Catholic Christian because "the Catholic Church is the structural and historical center of Christianity—not the whole, but the center."

The Church of which he is a member is very broadly defined. It is a spiritual Church including Protestants and non-Christians. "Are you a member of the institutional Catholic Church?" I asked. "Sort of—partly," he replied. It was not a solution for him, he said, to be simply the member of a spiritual church—there must be some social manifestation of his beliefs as well.

The transition from a Catholic college to a non-Catholic graduate school was important in the case of G.H. In college, which he attended while living at home in the East, he had been comfortable in his religion. When he found himself in graduate school, however, alone in a room, without social contacts or affiliation with a Church community, he began to ask questions for which the traditional answers proved inadequate.

Initially, his questioning was trouble-free, and he effortlessly drifted away from the Church. But when he decided to think seriously about leaving instead of just letting it happen, much anxiety arose.

All of his life he had regarded membership in the Church as dependent on an all-or-nothing acceptance of Catholic teaching. The turning point in his decision-making process was reached when he realized that an all-or-nothing, either-or proposition was not involved, that he could both remain in the Church and accept or reject what he wanted to.

What he rejects are the Assumption and "other silly doctrines," the current definition of the Eucharistic presence, the emphasis on personal sin, on obedience to authority, and on the superiority of the virgin state. "But, even after denying that, I find I am in what I consider the boundaries. I would have to do a whole lot to get out. I believe in the basics: Jesus Christ as Savior, etc. These place me in the Church."

T.T., a law student also employed with a law firm, is married and has one child. The son of wealthy parents whom he describes as "1938 liberal Catholics," he experienced no great upheaval concerning membership in the Church. Raised a Catholic, he had never looked for anything better. What change he had undergone, begun perhaps with some courses in his sophomore year of college, was gradual, "an independent examination of the faith." This examination, which he continues to pursue, has led him to believe the faith makes sense. His reasons for being a member of the Catholic Church are different now only in the sense that they are the product of reflection, whereas before they were the product of indoctrination.

The intensity of R.N.'s feelings made her interview particularly memorable. Raised Catholic by parents involved in ecumenical activity, she had never been trained to think in denominational terms. She reported experiencing religious crises over a long period of time, the most recent during her sophomore year of college when she became disenchanted with many of the institutional aspects of the Church. Undergoing "intense pressure," she thought about leaving, was leaning for a while toward atheism, and, several years later, is still not sure whether she wants to remain a Catholic, though she definitely wants to be a Christian. Certain religious experiences have made her wish to remain in the Church, as have a great sense of responsibility to the Catholic community and a deep friendship she shares with a seminarian. "There must be something to being Catholic if he is." Doctrine is not a terrible burden; it would never force her out of the Church because it can be reinterpreted and revitalized. As a theology student she hopes to participate in the revitalization; but, because she remains in a turmoil of indecision, she keeps open the door out of the Catholic Church. For the present, all she is sure of is "Loving is all there is."

Involvement with a young man was especially important in the case of E.M. After a summer in the Southwest as a lay missionary, she was about to join the order of nuns with whom she had been working. Advised by a priest to wait and think about it for a year, she went to Europe for her junior year of college. There she met and fell in love with Paul, a student in a similar program of study. Paul had a promising career in science ahead of him, but he was making plans to become a Protestant minister. The next year, her senior year in college, he entered the seminary.

Considering the possibility of continuing her relationship with him subjected E.M. to "as much anxiety as could be." While certain priests helped her work through her feelings, very few people, including the nuns at school and her parents, were sympathetic to her situation and able to give her support. She decided, however, that she could still work in the Church and share her life with Paul's. She would not only marry him, but enroll in the seminary at which he was studying.

As the first and only Catholic at the seminary, she is under constant pressure to rethink Catholicism and redefine what being a Catholic means to her. At present she believes in the basics of Church doctrine, but feels that teachings on infallibility, birth control, the sacraments, and indulgences have been poorly presented. She is quite sure her continuing presence at the seminary and her forthcoming marriage will foster more change in her feelings about Catholicism, but she does not foresee herself ever leaving the Catholic Church.

Being the only Catholic at a non-Catholic college one summer, "a real oddity on campus," and soon thereafter implicated in a drug and sex scandal, L.N. was plummeted into a thorough examination of herself. In the fall, she fell in with a group of "hippies and radicals" in the city where her Catholic college was located. This group, plus her interest in the civil rights movement and the work she did for community organizations, provided grist for the mill that revolved around the meaning of herself and her religion. More often committed to the Church than not, she had decided fairly well before coming to graduate school to remain a Catholic.

She came to graduate school a Wilson scholar and no longer a political radical. "It's something you grow out of." At the beginning of graduate school, she was again half out of the Church, this time because of the conservative Catholic center on campus and because local churches were behind the times. She met a group of students, however, who had a priest celebrate Mass regularly in their apartment. This apartment church proved to be supportive of her views, and she found it easy to remain in.

I asked her reasons for remaining a Catholic before coming to graduate school. "I couldn't find a better alternative," she related. "Either there is a God or there isn't. If there is, I have to act X way. Once I decided to believe in God, Catholicism seemed best, probably because I had been raised Catholic. Besides, the changing Church made it easier to be in."

Why believe in God? "The old Thomistic stuff: order in the world, structure in the world. It could not just have happened."

R.B. took the first steps toward change in her late twenties while she was still a nun. It was not a process, she said, of deciding whether to stay in or leave the Church. It was, rather, a process of understanding what the Church is: "The meaning of the Church changed, so there was not an IT to leave." Her transition took place, in conjunction with that of a number of other nuns, over a period of about a year, and involved very little crisis because "I knew a lot of theology and psychology."

Now no longer a nun or a "practicing Catholic in terms of Mass attendance, following the pope, etc., she says "I find in the Church the freedom to search for God and a meaningful relation with him. The Church might not consider me a member, but I do."

Both R.S. and her husband are lawyers. She would be attending Mass daily were it not for an infant daughter who keeps her confined at home.

Her reasons for being a member of the Church, she said, have not changed over the past ten years nor has she undergone any crisis about the faith. "When the questions appeared they would be answered easily." She was and is a member because "I believe in it as the true Church."

A problem with the Church, she said in the course of the interview, is the teachers and theologians who present their own ideas as doctrine instead of first teaching doctrine and then presenting their interpretation of it. "But that isn't a fault of the Church; it's a fault of those individuals." The Pope's encyclical on birth control she considers a "beautiful document." As far as Vatican II's statement on freedom of conscience goes, it was not a change of doctrine but a clarification of existing doctrine.

R.S. foresees no circumstances under which she would give up membership in the Catholic Church.

Other Ins mentioned as instigators of change: being free in the eighth grade to choose whether or not to attend Church; an excellent high school course in religion; encountering different kinds of Catholics while studying in Europe; a college course in the philosophy of God; exposure to other Catholics in college who were thinking the same things; involvement in liturgical change, and the concomitant necessity to learn more about the historical Church.

None of the fifty Ins reported they had ever left the Church only to return later. Two indicated they were "half in and half out" for a time, and eleven had "thought about leaving the Church." The majority (thirty-three), when asked about their experience of membership, checked the category "While I have never really thought about leaving the Church as a possibility for myself, my reasons for being a member have changed in the past ten years." Four responded: "My reasons for being a member of the Church have not changed in the past ten years." The bulk of re-evaluation, then, had to do with the meaning of membership rather than the desirability of membership.[2]

Those thirteen who had considered leaving said they were "getting away from the Church" more than "turning to something else." What they might have turned to was "humanism" or a "broad Christianity." Several mentioned that the Quakers (emphasis on peace) or the Unitarians (absence of dogma) had some appeal for them.[3]

In a number of instances, a religious figure, generally a priest, occasionally a nun, knew intimately of the process being experienced by the subject and was approving of it. This awareness was evident in the case of at least seventeen of the fifty Ins and is of interest because, while dissociating themselves from the institutional Church, these subjects, paradoxically, sought the counsel of an official representative of the institution.[4]

2. See Appendix II, p. 207, Question II.
3. See Appendix II, p. 210, Questions 13 and 14.
4. See Appendix II, p. 214, Question 18. Each protocol was inspected independently by two judges (one myself). If the subject's reply to Question 18 indicated "there was a religious figure who knew the subject personally, knew his position, was tolerant or approving of it, and conveyed this to the subject," the reply was scored "yes." The judges agreed 98 per cent of the time on this item. The one case over which they disagreed was placed in the "no" category. This procedure for coding open-ended material was followed on other data reported in this study.

Categorizing subjects' replies to "your reasons for being a member of the Church" proved extremely difficult. Asked for reasons *before* they changed, nearly everyone answered they had been born and raised Catholic and could not imagine an alternative. For reasons *after* they changed, nine subjects clearly indicated that the Church fit some personal value, need, or goal of theirs; seven listed a belief or hope in God and seven a belief or hope in Christ or the Church as one of their reasons. The majority of the responses to this open-ended question, however, had to be placed in the "other" category.[5]

When asked what was *gained* from membership, sixteen gave responses that could be clearly coded as "a sense of meaning to life," and fourteen "a sense of belonging to a community." Seven mentioned "security" or "peace of mind"; three said "nothing," two "contact with God or Christ." Eighteen mentioned various things that had to be coded "other." A number of subjects, of course, mentioned several of the above.[6]

What Ins felt they *lost* as members was chiefly independence of thought or action, this being mentioned by twelve. Ten noted other losses but the majority (twenty-eight) said "nothing."[7]

Finally, looking to the future, thirty Ins said they probably would never give up Catholicism although only fifteen foresaw no change in their present philosophy of life. Circumstances that would lead to abandoning Catholicism included both action on the Church's part, e.g., becoming more rigid

5. See Appendix II, p. 212, Questions 8 and 9. On "Reason before Change," the two judges agreed 98 per cent of the time. On "Reasons after Change," they agreed only 54 per cent of the time. All cases disagreed upon were placed in the "other" category.

6. See Appendix II, p. 216, Question 29. Agreement was 92 per cent; cases disagreed upon were placed in "other."

7. See Appendix II, p. 216, Question 30. Agreement was 86 per cent; cases disagreed upon were placed in "other."

or drawing more definite boundaries, and personal changes in one's state in life or one's outlook.[8]

Ten Outs

W.T. attended Mass daily through the latter part of grammar school and early high school. At one point he interviewed with the Christian Brothers, but never entered the order. In his sophomore year of college, aware of "philosophical, historical, and moral inconsistencies in the Church" and sensing "the gap between the rhetoric of the Church and what it practiced," he gave up Catholicism. But his leaving was "more an escape from my Irish-Italian environment. Lower middle class factory values are just not relevant to society at large."

Shortly thereafter the ecumenical movement in the Church caught his attention. Especially impressed by the Dutch theologians ("A radical conception of Catholicism became possible"), he returned to the Church. The hope of radical change in the Church soon faded, however. The ecumenical movement did not alter the basic structure of the Church; theologians he admired were held in disrepute, while the Church continued to hold up for emulation people like Pius XII who were more interested in maintaining the institution than seeing the Church practice what it preached. Also, the question of religion and the existence of God was becoming irrelevant to him.

His ambivalence about the Church, protracted over a period of time, was heightened when he became engaged to a girl who was a fervent Catholic (they did not marry). In his first year of graduate school he consciously and deliberately

8. See Appendix II, p. 216, Questions 31 to 35. On Question 34 agreement was 90 per cent; cases disagreed upon were placed in a combination category.

did not make his Easter duty, this signifying to him that he had left the Church for good.

Previously, he felt rage toward the Church and betrayed it. After his final departure, he felt "released from tensions that were not creative" and more honest in his personal relations. Now a "radical humanist" who finds it easier to be a Christian outside the Church than in it, he is involved in radical political action on campus.

He did not make the move alone. His five closest friends, all "lower middle class, urban," are, like himself, "escaped Catholic intellectuals."

By all outward signs a practicing Catholic, A.G. rejects so much of the Church that he cannot call himself in without being a hypocrite. All he can accept about the Church is its basic message, but, unfortunately, the Church is not even loyal to that.

Having grown up in a lower class neighborhood, he felt marginal in college to the middle class Catholic community. Courses in college presented the faith in a way so he would question it. "Trying to answer the questions got me where I am." He never actually "left" the Church, he said, but feels as though he is out.

The underground Church is not an alternative for him. These middle class, young liberal elite have "a snobbish holier-than-thou attitude." They say they are critical of the faith when really they are not. They have cut themselves off from the parishes, which may be comforting for them, but certainly unhealthy for the parishes. They are less Christian than the old lady Catholics.

As a sociology student who wants to work to alleviate poverty, he sees the Church in some countries withholding vast resources from the poor. "They say they are helping to fight poverty, but they aren't. In Chicago racial prejudice is essentially Catholic. The Church cannot even persuade its own members to be Christian."

If there were a group of Catholics with whom he could identify, he might after a year or so return to Catholicism. Presently, though, he only performs the externals, because of habit, because his wife is a firm Catholic, and because he thinks it necessary to provide some religious upbringing for his child. If he were absolutely sure he wished to be out, even the external practice would cease.

"Let's say I've taken an extended leave of absence," was the way R.O. described his position regarding membership in the Church. He said he wanted to be a member of the Church and he wanted to believe in God more firmly, but he just could not do so at present.

Several years ago, while studying psychology at another graduate school, he began to have doubts about his own immortality. The doubts grew when he came to law school in Chicago, where attending Mass made him feel more and more aloof from the Church. To overcome his doubts and his aloofness he tried more frequent religious practice, making a retreat and beginning to attend daily Mass. The doubts about immortality, however, soon developed into nightmares about death. Immortality had been an anchor point of belief in college: "I could not imagine myself not existing." But now he had a terrible fear of dying. As soon as he decided to stop attending Church, he felt an immediate sense of relief.

He indicated his fear of death is now resolved, although he is still uncertain about his belief in immortality. The same is true of his belief in God. "You just cannot say one way or the other."

A sense of apathy and ennui regarding immortality and God has since developed. He is just "indifferent to taking a risk in believing in something that might not exist." This detachment has influenced other areas of his life as well. "I can't buckle down to anything; I'm afraid to make a commitment—to law, to a girl, to anything." His apathy, an "unexplainable drift" he cannot understand or control, has moved him to seek help at the student medical health center.

As far as beliefs are concerned, he said he is, in the main, a Catholic. His moral behavior has not changed since leaving. Often he finds himself defending the Church in discussion, and he attends Mass when he is with his family. But he is still on a "leave of absence" to allow himself the time and freedom to think things out, first his own personal problem and then his problem with the Church.

Six months after the interview, R.O. wrote that he was unable to determine whether he was in or out of the Church and that his own personal crisis had heightened.

J.R. was active in college in seeking the liberalization of the Church. He was part of the Student Christian Movement, editor of an ecumenical journal, and a participant in some of the first experimental Masses. He planned at one time to become a Jesuit priest.

He says now that "I simply liberalized myself out of the Church." A catalyst in the process was his engagement to a Quaker girl from an anti-Catholic family (they never married). He reached the point of decision during an ecumenical summer project in the inner city, where at Mass one Sunday he was struck by the "oldness of forms." They no longer had any meaning for him, and he decided on the spot that he could no longer be a Catholic. The decision was made with little anxiety, though it later caused tension at home.

It was Christianity that he left, not just the Catholic Church. "There was enough latitude in the Catholic Church to be a Christian in it if I wanted to." It wasn't that the Church was rigid—he thought of it as loose and flexible; it was, rather, that religious traditions as a whole do not come to terms with contemporary social situations.

"To look back in time to find the meaning of present events is inadequate and irrelevant. You need new solutions to new problems." Those friends of his "who reinterpret in the Christian tradition are somewhat dishonest. They take modern insights and then go back and say they find it in the words of Jesus."

His chief concerns now are social problems. He is interested in social theories and political philosophy and is immersed in Kant and Hegel. He is also looking for "a new way of being religious, of understanding man."

J.A. was baptized shortly after birth, although his father was not a Catholic and his mother practiced irregularly. He never attended a Catholic grammar school or a Catholic high school. In his senior year of high school, however, he began thinking seriously about religious and ethical problems. By the time he was a freshman at a Catholic college, he was experiencing strong religious inclinations, something he had never known before.

But in his junior year of college he stopped going to Mass. "I had left the Church as a legislative body earlier, but I quit going to Mass because of an intellectual decision to be an atheist."

Now he still considers himself an atheist, a "philosopher of the absurd." He feels no antagonism toward religion or Catholicism and would like to teach philosophy at a Catholic college and make the people he contacts "more ethically and morally aware."

F.K. attended Mass daily throughout most of her school years. Then at graduate school she became involved in a love affair with one of her professors, intelligent and an atheist. A "traumatic" period ensued. She was faced with a clear-cut choice between "the whole Catholic framework—belief in God, sexual morality and the guilt associated with it—and a love relationship with this man."

Too tired to make both work and to worry about guilt and sin, she chose the love relationship. An adult sexual involvement seemed much more satisfying than her relationship with the Church. Ed made her feel intelligent, worthwhile, a woman; he replaced those things the Church had done for her. She stopped going to Sunday Mass. "God became irrelevant."

Three months later the affair was over, but F.K. was surprised that she didn't need to return to the Church. She left graduate school after the first year and became a mental health worker. Now she has no faith other than "living as a human being fully and taking one day at a time." Support for her feelings comes from her place of work, where both her supervisor, whom she admires greatly, and nearly all her fellow trainees are ex-Catholics. "The patients are all Catholics, the staff all ex-Catholics."

She feels she has gained "a more comfortable attitude toward life, a chance to see myself without judging myself." She regrets her loss of the ability to be honest with her family and a sense of oneness with them. In the future, she may miss a spiritual element to life, but she feels no such emptiness now.

Would she ever return to Catholicism? "I don't think so. I might like to—in some respects it would make life easier. It would be like tying myself to my roots again. But I have seen so many holes in it.

"I might like a Church wedding. I haven't told my family yet, which means that being out isn't finalized."

"I lacked faith all along," said B.G. "I never internalized Catholic beliefs in the first place." She recalled wanting in grammar school to delay her first confession and communion because of doubts. She remembered nuns who taught children to depreciate themselves and who instilled fear in them. She spoke of being jealous of students in the public schools who were able to study science when she could not. Several times as she grew up, she had thoughts about not being Catholic, but she continued to go to Mass.

In college the doubts became "stronger, more philosophical, and more specific." She experienced a "great deal of anxiety" over a long period of time, and it wasn't until a year after graduation, when she attended "a really bizarre Mass" in a mission church, that she finally decided to leave the Church.

Summing up her reasons for leaving, she cited "extravagant doctrinal claims, a hypocritical attitude toward the poor, and ridiculous doctrines on birth control and sex." "The Catholic Church," she remarked, "is cluttered with nonessentials."

Two years later, she finds herself relieved, not so hard on herself, but still bound in a number of ways to the Church. She reads three Catholic magazines regularly and has read a number of books on religion and Catholicism. If she married and had children, "I would feel guilty if I ignored my background and denied its influence. I would want my kids exposed to what is good in Catholicism."

S.S. grew up a Catholic in an all Protestant town. Her mother rarely attended church. Her father converted to Catholicism when she was ten, practiced regularly for three or four years, "wanted to believe in it, but couldn't." She chose a Catholic college at the suggestion of her older sister and because she herself was developing an interest in religion.

In college her "good Catholic" older sister began living with a man and became vehemently anti-Church. Still S.S. could not condemn her sister; it seemed obvious that she was becoming a better person because of the relationship. S.S. then met Richard, began a serious relationship with him, and found their thinking with respect to the Church to be very similar.

As for the Catholic college, it turned out to be opposite to what she naively expected it to be. Theology and philosophy courses were terrible. A number of the priest-professors were alcoholics. The "good Catholic girls" in her dormitory were repulsive to her. Her experience at this college, "the best thing that happened to me," made her come to grips with the Church and turn away from it.

Now married to Richard, who is also out of the Church, she finds herself, unfortunately, surrounded at work by more of these "good Catholic girls." My interview was an opportunity, she said, to tell her side of the story.

"I have a hang-up about saying I have left the Church. The problem is not in me but in the Church. If *it* would become relevant I would latch on again."

"There are two Churches right now," J.O. continued. "I am not affiliated with the traditional Church. And I am not really aligned with the bastard or schismatic Church, but sort of interested in it. I would be interested in a coalition, but I don't think the two Churches will ever get together. If there were hope for a coalition, I would be in."

The old traditional Church is too much like Dick Daley, the new underground Church a little like the Yippies. She is more a Gene McCarthy but finds no group in the Church like him, although she hasn't looked too much.

She never thought consciously about leaving; the Church just became more and more irrelevant. She had been an ardent Catholic, a daily communicant, thinking "I was somebody special by being Catholic." This feeling persisted until early adulthood when she was faced with a concrete ethical decision and found "I could honestly say I didn't know right from wrong—and I thought I would know." The old clichés of Catholicism just did not work.

Her re-evaluation, involving a "hell of a lot of pressure," led her to realize that her Catholic background had taken her away from people rather than led her toward them. "The Catholic schools set up a caste system, cutting you off from Protestants, Jews, and blacks." They set up a rigid definition of the best way to live. It was hard for her to get out and realize other people were just as good.

Her leaving Catholicism was not a departure from Christianity nor an abandonment of the spiritual life. It made no difference in her moral outlook. It meant, rather, the beginning of real contemplation and of a pure relation with God, since all rules and regulations were now out of the picture.

J.O. was ambiguous about the permanency of her position outside the Church. At times she spoke of it as a sabbatical, as a chance to reassess herself. She spoke of a need to go back in and contribute to whatever progress was taking place. "I feel a lot of us who have fallen away for a time will go back and try to work in the system."

While teaching religion in a Catholic high school, B.Y. used to think up provocative questions for her students. The questions had the unexpected effect, however, of forcing *her* into a serious examination of Catholicism, and the answers she arrived at were hardly satisfactory. "By the end of the year I was out of my mind. What could I tell my students without being a hypocrite?"

Her husband, an ex-seminarian, was already leaving the Church, and his challenging of her positions was a major influence. Within a year she stopped attending Sunday Mass ("There was nothing more meaningless"), and no matter how much she thought being a Catholic was not commensurate with attending Mass, she realized the Church defined being Catholic in that way. Consequently, when she stopped attending Mass, she felt she had left the Church.

She had stayed in for a long time, she said, because to her the institutional Church was not the real Church. But, in the end, she was "overwhelmed by the immovability and power of the institution." It was rich and people were starving. It was identified with the power structure in places where people were oppressed by the power structure. "It's absolutely fossilized in its own formalism." She decided the institutional Church was the real Church, and she could no longer be a part of it.

She became agnostic for a time, but now calls herself "a wandering Christian confused about where to hitch up."

There was great diversity in the kinds of events that started people on the way out: a high school religion teacher who considered atheism a valid possibility; a sensitivity training group; a parent who argued against Catholicism; a nervous breakdown in a "religiously fanatic" friend; Vatican II, which exposed much corruption in the Church; Catholic relatives who were racially prejudiced and felt it was "my country—right or wrong"; poor, irrelevant sermons; "brutal, insensitive" religious instructors; encountering non-Catholics; meeting other Catholic students going through the same thing ("It was *in* to be agnostic"); a baby who made attendance at church too much trouble. College courses, generally very good ones or very bad ones, were mentioned quite often as catalysts.

Only fifteen Outs reported a definite decision to leave; the others simply found themselves out. A "concrete act by which you gave up membership" was, in forty cases, ceasing to attend Mass and/or the sacraments. In two cases it was something else, and in eight there was no such concrete sign that one was out.[9]

Twenty-six subjects said their leaving was more getting away from the Church than turning to something else. Fifteen said they were actually turning to something else, and nine could not characterize their leaving either way. The most frequent response to "what you have changed to" was "no religion, though not atheist" (eighteen). Sixteen answered "a

9. See Appendix II, p. 218, Questions 8 and 9.

personal religion, with no affiliation with any religious group";
eight chose "a broad Christianity"; five "no religion, atheist";
two "a broad Catholicism." One subject could not decide. In
the open-ended part of this question, several subjects indicated
they had turned to some kind of humanism. No one had taken
up another religion.[10]

As with the Ins, there were a number of instances (seventeen clearly identified) in which a religious figure knew of and
was tolerant of approving of the process being undergone by
the Out subject. Again, in the course of dissociation from an
institution, an official representative of the institution was on
hand to witness or take part in the process. This attachment
bespeaks a subtle kind of dependence on the very thing one is
attempting to gain freedom from.[11]

In the case of twenty-five subjects, "your reasons for leaving the Church" could be described in part as "found the
Church or its doctrine irrelevant and/or meaningless." Twenty
included reasons more purely intellectual: they could not believe all or part of Church doctrine. Seven said they were re-
pelled by characteristics of the institutional Church and six
by the Church's handling of social issues. The above was in
reply to an open-ended question.[12]

What the Outs *gained* by leaving was chiefly "independence
of thought or action" (mentioned by twenty-five). Seven included "peace of mind" and seven "honesty" or "less hypocrisy." Fourteen said something that had to be coded "other,"
and four replied "nothing."[13]

The chief *loss* was "security," "certitude," or "stability"
(mentioned by seventeen). Twenty-three sensed that nothing

10. See Appendix II, p. 219, Questions 13 to 15.
11. See Appendix II, p. 220, Question 18. Agreement was 96 per
cent; the two cases disagreed upon were coded "No."
12. See Appendix II, p. 218, Question 10. Agreement was 72 per
cent; cases disagreed upon were placed in "other."
13. See Appendix II, p. 222, Question 29. Agreement was 77 per
cent; cases disagreed upon were placed in "other."

was lost. Five mentioned "a sense of belonging to a community." There were five "others."[14]

"Do you think you will ever change back to Catholicism?" elicited two yes's among the Outs, twenty flat no's, and twenty-eight replies classified "other." There was slightly more openness to change in the Outs' present philosophy of life. Ten foresaw a change; seventeen foresaw none and twenty-three replies were classified "other." A change in the circumstances of one's personal life was mentioned more often as a possible reason for returning to the Church than was a change in the Church, but both possibilities were frequently brought up.[15]

Summary: A Totally Ambiguous Situation

After listening to one hundred of these stories, I became aware that one's position of being in or out of the Church was not arrived at on the basis of what might be called empirical evidence, for the same evidence could be and was acknowledged by both Ins and Outs. Both Ins and Outs pointed out unacceptable or irrelevant doctrines; both mentioned racism among Catholics; both regarded with disdain the formalism, pomp, and circumstance of the hierarchy. The Outs, identifying these characteristics with the Catholic Church, no longer wished to be a part of the Church. The Ins, however, generally redefined the Catholic Church in a way compatible with their beliefs and considered these undesirable characteristics as only one element of the Church, an element they dissociated themselves from. Why would the Ins go through the effort of redefining "Catholic Church," and why would not the Outs?

14. See Appendix II, p. 222, Question 30. Agreement was 90 per cent; cases disagreed upon were placed in "other."
15. See Appendix II, p. 222, Questions 31–35. On Question 34, agreement was 90 per cent; cases disagreed upon were placed in "other."

It does not appear to be a question of knowledge of the Church. The Outs were aware of diverse elements in the Church, but still perceived it in one particular way. To redefine the Church in order to remain in would be, they felt, dishonest or hypocritical. "I extended the meaning of the Church," said one, "until it could no longer be extended." The Ins, on the other hand, looked at undesirable elements in the Church as something to be changed. According to them, to leave the Church would be abandoning the ship in its time of need, a "cop-out."

The point is that the "evidence" could be construed in a number of ways. Which way it was construed seemed more a question of wanting than a question of seeing. It began to appear from the interviews that one almost chose to see the Church and one's relation to it in a certain way. There was, in other words, some a-rational starting point that distinguished Ins from Outs, a point from which all the definitions of the Church, all the positions with regard to doctrine, and all the construing of evidence about the Church's social and political life seemed to follow.

The question became, then: what was the determinant of that a-rational want? What made one person view an ambiguous, fluid set of beliefs, values, and information about the Church and see one structure emerging, while someone else viewed the same set of beliefs, values, and information and saw a different structure emerging? The answer seemed to lie in the web of interpersonal relationships in which these people were situated, in the past as well as in the present. Their social psychology appeared to come to the surface as they described the ambiguous stimulus that was the Catholic Church.

But to say that is to press the search for why prematurely. It is first necessary to turn to the description of groups and see more accurately what Ins and Outs believe, what they value, and how they perceive the Catholic Church.

PART II

The Results of Change

FOUR

What They Believe

Midway through the two-hour interview that provided the basic data of this study, each subject was given a list of twenty Catholic belief formulas and asked to indicate his position with respect to them on a seven-point scale ranging from "Definitely False" to "Definitely True." All the beliefs were phrased in a positive manner, so that agreement with them would indicate the subject was orthodox in his beliefs and disagreement that he was unorthodox. Positive and negative items were not counterbalanced because meaningful opposites to most of the beliefs could not be written. Besides, it seemed more important to obtain a subject's acceptance or rejection of the beliefs as those beliefs had been presented to him earlier in life, i.e., in a positive fashion.

Most of the items were phrased quite simply, reading like excerpts from the Baltimore catechism. Some subjects objected to this phrasing, but most realized that items that were to be commented on by one hundred different people had to be plainly worded. If a subject insisted that a statement had to be qualified before he could agree or disagree, he was told to respond closer to the center of the scale.

The twenty beliefs fell into two major categories and a number of subcategories or types. Ten of the beliefs were designed to deal with "Man and This World." Five of these were statements about the nature of man ("has free will," "has an immortal soul," etc.), and five were statements about morality ("premarital sexual intercourse is morally wrong," "abortion is morally wrong," etc.). The other ten beliefs were designed to deal with "God and the Other World," including items about the Church itself, the intersection, it is believed, between God and man. Two of these ten beliefs dealt with God, two with Christ, two with Mary, two with the afterlife, and two with the Church. These categories were not meant to be hard and fast pigeonholes, but rather indicators of the general nature of a belief.

Several things should be kept in mind when interpreting subjects' responses to these beliefs. First of all, there is more than one meaning to the zero point on the response scale. In the concrete, a zero reply often did correspond in meaning to the zero point's label "No position one way or the other," but just as often it meant "Who cares?" or "If you mean X, I would say +3, but if you mean Y, I would say −3." In other words, it meant the subject was apathetic about the belief (as often happened with beliefs about Mary), or it meant the subject was ambivalent about the belief, usually because it was expressed too simply (as often happened with the belief about abortion).

If the meaning of a reply in the center of the scale was obscure, the meaning of a reply on either extreme was quite clear. It meant only one thing: that the subject clearly accepted (+3, "Definitely True") or rejected (−3, "Definitely False") this particular formulation of the belief.

In view of the above, In-Out differences lying near the extremes of the scale are easier to interpret and of greater importance than In-Out differences hovering around the center. A distinction should be drawn, then, between differences that are *statistically significant* and ones that are *meaningful*. For example, a mean difference of two points in the center of the scale (which would turn out to be statistically significant) is not nearly as meaningful as a difference of two points nearer the extremes of the scale. "Possibly False (−1)" and "Possibly True (+1)" are not mutually exclusive even though there is a difference of two scale points between them. Indeed, logically they say the same thing: if something is possibly false, it is also possibly true. To be consistent with positions taken earlier, though, an In might say "Possibly True" in this realm of the possible and an Out "Possibly False." "Definitely True (+3)" and "Possibly True (+1)," however, representing the same scale difference of two points, are much more *meaningfully* distinct. Hence, in looking at In-Out differences in beliefs, we should be impressed not only by the magnitude of the statistical difference but by where on the scale the difference is located.

With this in mind, the reader can inspect Figure 4.1 and Table 4.1 to see what Ins and Outs believe and what the differences between them are. Statistically, all the differences but one are significant at the .05 level or better. We should note, however, that the average In reply to the items fluctuated around "Possibly True" and the average Out reply around "Possibly False," responses near the center of the scale.

Figure 4.1 and Table 4.1 arrange the beliefs in order of their *F* values, which indicate the degree to which the beliefs discriminate between Ins and Outs. Thus, the best discriminants are at the top of the list and the poorest at the bottom. Generally, the beliefs relating to "God and the Other World" are the better discriminants, the top seven being of this kind. The poorer discriminants are the "Man and This World" items, the bottom eight being from this category. Why one kind of belief should be a better discriminant than another will be discussed later.

What Ins Accept

A typical In belief system could be constructed by looking at those beliefs that Ins are most certain of. Taking the beliefs

Figure 4.1. In-Out differences in the acceptance of twenty beliefs. The bar represents the size of the mean In-Out difference. Items are arranged in order of F values (See Table 4.1).

Type		Definitely False −3	Probably False −2	Possibly False −1	No Position One Way or the Other 0	Possibly True +1	Probably True +2	Definitely True +3
Christ	5. Christ rose from the dead.			Outs				Ins
Christ	15. Christ is really present in the Eucharist.			Outs				Ins
God	13. There are three Persons in one God.			Outs			Ins	
Church	11. The pope is infallible when speaking on matters of faith and morals.		Outs		Ins			
Church	1. The Catholic Church is the one true Church.		Outs			Ins		
God	3. There is a God.					Outs		Ins
Afterlife	9. There is a state of eternal reward called heaven.			Outs			Ins	
Man	18. Every man is born with original sin.			Outs		Ins		
Man	6. Every man has an immortal, spiritual soul.				Outs			Ins

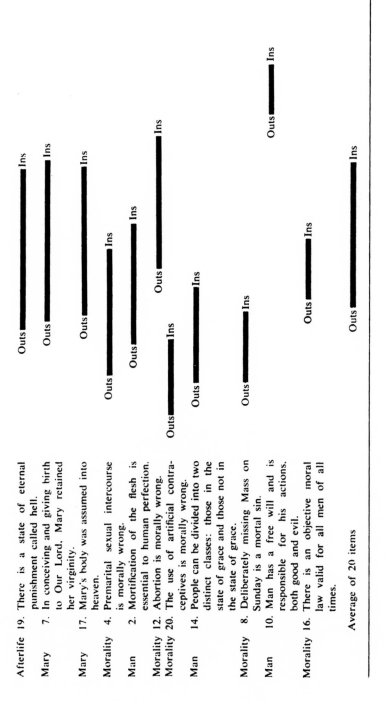

Table 4.1. In-Out Difference in the Acceptance of Twenty Beliefs

Belief No. and Type		Mean Ins	Mean Outs	Mean In-Out Diff.	F	p<
5	Christ	2.58	− .96	3.54	236.59	.0001
15	Christ	2.32	− .96	3.28	153.76	.0001
13	God	2.02	−1.06	3.08	126.43	.0001
11	Church	.54	−2.22	2.76	84.70	.0001
1	Church	.96	−2.06	3.02	78.71	.0001
3	God	2.78	.98	1.80	76.66	.0001
9	Afterlife	1.88	− .72	2.60	71.94	.0001
18	Man	1.36	−1.32	2.68	67.57	.0001
6	Man	2.32	.10	2.22	63.32	.0001
19	Afterlife	.78	−1.76	2.54	58.78	.0001
7	Mary	.86	−1.54	2.40	55.07	.0001
17	Mary	.80	−1.38	2.18	51.38	.0001
4	Morality	− .32	−2.22	1.90	34.04	.0001
2	Man	.02	−1.82	1.84	23.62	.0001
12	Morality	1.14	− .68	1.82	22.56	.0001
20	Morality	−1.78	−2.74	.96	16.31	.0002
14	Man	− .98	−2.30	1.32	15.54	.0002
8	Morality	−1.24	−2.36	1.12	11.04	.0013
10	Man	2.32	1.70	.62	5.31	.0234
16	Morality	− .30	−1.04	.74	2.52	.1159
Average of 20 items		.90	−1.22	2.12	159.33	.0001

Note: Items are arranged in order of *F* values, which indicate the degree to which the distribution of In scores is different from the distribution of Out scores. For the full wording of each item, see Figure 4.1.

that have a mean score of +2 ("Probably True") or above and arranging them in terms of the certitude felt about them by Ins, we can determine what is the bedrock of most In belief systems:

There is a God.　(+2.78)

Christ rose from the dead.　(+2.58)

Christ is really present in the Eucharist.   (+2.32)

Man has a free will and is responsible for his actions, both good and evil.   (+2.32)

Every man has an immortal, spiritual soul.   (+2.32)

There are three Persons in one God.   (+2.02)

Four of these are of the "God and the Other World" type. One of the two about man deals indirectly with the other world ("immortal soul"), and the other ("free will") is generally assented to whether one is In or Out.

What Ins Reject

Earlier in the interview, an open-ended question was put to Ins, "Are there any teachings or doctrines of the Church that you find especially unattractive or false?" Twenty-five of fifty spontaneously mentioned birth control, fifteen said papal infallibility, and thirteen mentioned teachings having to do with Mary. Also included in some lists were teachings on celibacy and virginity (in seven), on sin and confession (in six), on the afterlife (in five), and on divorce (in four). Nine subjects listed a variety of other doctrines and six found no doctrines especially unattractive or false.[1]

Responding to the set belief formulas of the present section, In subjects reject most the teaching on birth control. The five items having negative means, none of which are as strong as "Probably False," are:

The use of artificial contraceptives is morally wrong. (−1.78)

1. See Appendix II, p. 215, Question 26. Agreement between the two judges was 98 per cent; cases disagreed upon were placed in "Other."

Deliberately missing Mass on Sunday is a mortal sin.
(−1.24)

People can be divided into two distinct classes: those
in the state of grace and those not in the state of grace.
(−.98)

Premarital sexual intercourse is morally wrong.
(−.32)

There is an objective moral law valid for all men of
all times.   (−.30)

All of these beliefs are of the "Man and This World" type,
and four of them have to do with morality.

What Outs Accept

Paralleling a question put to Ins, it was asked of Outs if
there were "any teachings or doctrines of the Church that you
find especially attractive or true?" Roughly half (twenty-three)
of the Outs said "No" or "Nothing exclusively Catholic." The
idea of love, often as portrayed in the life of Jesus in the
Gospels, was mentioned as attractive by fourteen. Two mentioned papal social teachings, and the remainder came up with
other or unspecifiable teachings.[2]

As far as the set beliefs in the present section go, there are
three for which the mean Out score is positive:

Man has a free will and is responsible for his actions,
both good and evil.   (+1.70)

There is a God.   (+.98)

Every man has an immortal, spiritual soul.   (+.10)

---

2. See Appendix II, p. 221, Question 26. Agreement between the
two judges was 87 per cent; cases disagreed upon were placed in
"Other."

These are all beliefs for which mean In scores are above $+2$. The Ins, of course, are more firm in their acceptance of them.

What Outs Reject

Reversing what was done for Ins, we can list in order the beliefs Outs say most certainly are false. Those beliefs with means below -2 ("Probably False")" are:

The use of artificial contraceptives is morally wrong. (-2.74)

Deliberately missing Mass on Sunday is a mortal sin. (-2.36)

People can be divided into two distinct classes: those in the state of grace and those not in the state of grace. (-2.30)

Premarital sexual intercourse is morally wrong. (-2.22)

The pope is infallible when speaking on matters of faith and morals. (-2.22)

The Catholic Church is the one true Church. (-2.06)

The first four of these are the same beliefs most rejected by Ins. The position of Ins on the last two are between "No Position" and "Possibly True": they neither accept nor reject them. The conclusion seems warranted, then, that Ins and Outs object to the same beliefs, but Outs are more firm in their rejection of them.

Extreme Cases Among Ins and Outs

Figure 4.1 and Table 4.1 revealed those beliefs *most likely* to be found among Ins and among Outs. Figure 4.2 depicts

Figure 4.2. Beliefs of most rejecting Ins and most accepting Outs. For each item, the mean of the 5 most negative In scores and the mean of the 5 most positive Out scores were calculated. The bar represents the size of the difference between these means. The figure indicates the beliefs it is possible to find associated with being in or being out.

Type		Definitely False −3	Probably False −2	Possibly False −1	No Position One Way or the Other 0	Possibly True +1	Probably True +2	Definitely True +3
						Mean of 5 most positive Outs		
					Mean of 5 most negative Ins			
Christ	5. Christ rose from the dead.				…Ins ▭ …Outs			
Christ	15. Christ is really present in the Eucharist.				…Ins ▭ …Outs			
God	13. There are three Persons in one God.		…Ins ▭ …Outs					
Church	11. The pope is infallible when speaking on matters of faith and morals.	…Ins ▭ …Outs						
Church	1. The Catholic Church is the one true Church.	…Ins ▭ …Outs						
God	3. There is a God.					…Ins ▭ …Outs		
Afterlife	9. There is a state of eternal reward called heaven.			…Ins ▭ …Outs				
Man	18. Every man is born with original sin.		…Ins ▭ …Outs					
Man	6. Every man has an immortal, spiritual soul.				…Ins ▭ …Outs			

Afterlife 19. There is a state of eternal punishment called hell.

Mary 7. In conceiving and giving birth to Our Lord, Mary retained her virginity.

Mary 17. Mary's body was assumed into heaven.

Morality 4. Premarital sexual intercourse is morally wrong.

Man 2. Mortification of the flesh is essential to human perfection.

Morality 12. Abortion is morally wrong.

Morality 20. The use of artificial contraceptives is morally wrong.

Man 14. People can be divided into two distinct classes: those in the state of grace and those not in the state of grace.

Morality 8. Deliberately missing Mass on Sunday is a mortal sin.

Man 10. Man has a free will and is responsible for his actions, both good and evil.

Morality 16. There is an objective moral law valid for all men of all times.

Average of 20 items

... Ins ... Outs

beliefs *it is possible* to find among each of these two groups. For each belief item, the five most positive Out scores were averaged, as were the five most negative In scores, to give some idea of the range of In and Out positions and to point out that In-Out status, while being a fair indicator of a person's beliefs, is no absolute guarantor of them. That a whole range of beliefs is available to Ins and Outs also increases a sense of the seeming arbitrariness of one's In-Out status.

Similarities and Differences

Ins and Outs are alike in that a particular belief formula evokes similar reactions from each group. There is a Spearman correlation of $+.866$ ($p < .01$, 1-tailed) between the order in which Ins accept the list of beliefs and the order in which Outs do. That is, items that Ins are more approving of Outs are also more approving of, and items that Ins are more likely to reject Outs are also more likely to reject. The difference between the two groups is that Outs are, on the average, 2.12 scale points more negative than Ins. Thus, beliefs that Ins most strongly agree with Outs are close to taking no position on, while beliefs that Outs most strongly disagree with Ins generally take no position on. Overall, Ins are positive toward fifteen beliefs and Outs are positive toward three.

While nearly all items discriminate between Ins and Outs, some are better discriminants than others. An item's discriminatory power is only somewhat independent of whether it is accepted or rejected (the Spearman rho correlation between the order in which items discriminate Ins and Outs and the order in which Ins accept the items is $+.617$ [$p < .01$, 1-tailed]), and the correlation between the discriminatory order and the order in which Outs accept items is $+.223$ (N.S.). Those seven items that are the best discriminants are of the "God and the Other World" type. Those eight that are the poorest are of the "Man and This World" type. Why should one kind of item discriminate better than another?

One point of distinction between these two broad categories of beliefs is their accessibility to common experiential evidence. This evidence may derive originally from psychology, sociology, anthropology, or other social sciences, but more likely it is simply the evidence about life garnered by doing nothing else than growing up and living it. Human experiences common to men in this world can lead to similar conclusions about this kind of belief, conclusions either in line with traditional Catholic positions (e.g., free will) or at odds with them (e.g., original sin, birth control, premarital sex). It does not seem as likely, however, that one will encounter common tangible evidence that either contradicts or confirms other-worldly beliefs such as the existence of God, the Trinity, Christ's presence in the Eucharist, and so on. Hence, Ins and Outs are freer to vary with respect to these beliefs.

The first question to ask about one of these positively phrased beliefs, then, is: *can* it be contradicted by common experiential evidence? Generally, beliefs about "God and the Other World" cannot, and they turn out to be the best discriminants between Ins and Outs, the Ins accepting them and the Outs rejecting them. If the belief *can* be contradicted, as is the case with beliefs about "Man and This World," the next question is: *is* it contradicted? If the answer is yes, both Ins and Outs will tend to reject it; and if the answer is No, both will tend to continue accepting it. In either case, the item distinguishes less well between Ins and Outs.

We find, then, that the more ambiguous beliefs are the ones that separate Ins and Outs, ambiguous as defined by the fact that no tangible evidence open to a community of observers relates to them, and ambiguous as evidenced by the fact that Ins and Outs respond to them in quite different ways. Why should Ins respond one way to the ambiguity and Outs another way?

A theologian might say "faith," meaning a gift from God given to Ins to help them accept the beliefs and withheld from Outs, leading to their rejection of them. (Indeed, the ambiguous "God and the Other World" beliefs would be placed by traditional Catholicism in the category of "faith" as opposed to that of "morals.") The answer may also be faith in a non-theological sense: the Ins might be less complex, less questioning, and simply more inclined to accept such propositions. The fact that Ins and Outs were taken from the same graduate school population joins with my own impressions from conducting the interviews to reject the latter explanation, while the former is useless in the present analysis.

The simplest and most plausible explanation derives from the laws of cognitive consistency, laws that seem to be more telling when they deal with ambiguous objects of cognition. Ins find themselves positively associated with the Church, find the Church accepting the beliefs, and so themselves accept the beliefs, especially since there is no concrete evidence contradicting them. Outs, on the other hand, find themselves dissociated from the Church that accepts the beliefs, and so they become dissociated from the beliefs, especially since there is no concrete evidence confirming them. In the absence of common experiential evidence, wanting or not wanting to be a member of the Catholic Church can exert a strong pull or push on what one believes.

The Church would also exert a greater pull or push on those beliefs it showed a united front on. Ins, for example, might feel they could take or leave certain beliefs the Church itself is ambiguous about, while feeling they must believe those that the Church is clear about. Outs, if they were truly dissociated from the Church, would reject most those beliefs the Church showed a united front on, and reject less the ones the Church was vague about. In other words, if membership in the Church exerts an influence on whether one accepts or rejects ambiguous beliefs, the influence will be more strongly felt if the link between the Church and the belief is unequivocal.

A measure of how united the Church appears to be on each of the twenty beliefs is contained in Table 6.4. In the part of the questionnaire referred to there, Ins and Outs indicated what they thought was the thinking of the Church on each of the twenty belief formulas. Those beliefs on which their replies are in closer agreement must be the ones the Church is clearer about.

Table 6.4 lists the beliefs in order of their ability to discriminate In and Out estimates of the "thinking of the Church." If the reasoning expressed above is correct, we would expect a negative correlation between the order in which the beliefs appear in Table 6.4 and the order in which they appear in Table 4.1. That is, the beliefs the Church is clearest about (those near the bottom of Table 6.4) should be the ones that best distinguish In and Out reports of what they themselves believe (those near the top of Table 4.1).

The Spearman rank-order correlation between the two lists of beliefs is $-.502$ ($p < .05$, 1-tailed), and the rank-order correlation between lists of the ten "God and the Other World" beliefs is $-.522$ ($p < .06$, 1-tailed), indicating support for the above analysis. The support is qualified, however, because the poorest discriminants in Table 6.4 are not all of the "God and the Other World" type.

In response to the question of why some belief formulas discriminate better than others, then, we have suggested that beliefs about "Man and This World" discriminate less well because there is a pool of common evidence relating to them that is available to both Ins and Outs. Those ambiguous beliefs about "God and the Other World" are better discriminants because, in the absence of such common evidence, one's membership ties exert a strong influence on what one believes. There is also some substantiation for the proposition that this influence is augmented when the Church shows a united front on a particular belief.

This explanation need not assume (as might be implied above) that, because membership is associated with belief, membership determines belief. It could be the other way around, i.e., one might be personally convinced of some belief that we have called ambiguous, and this conviction might lead him to be a member of the Church. A third explanation, perhaps the most conservative, is that some a-rational want determines both membership and belief. In any case, we find that one's membership status is an important factor relating to how one reacts to ambiguous beliefs about God and the other world.

Summary

In response to the basic question this chapter asks, what beliefs best distinguish Ins and Outs in both a statistical and a meaningful sense, we can point to the six items at the top of Figure 4.1 and Table 4.1. Two are beliefs about Christ, two about God, and two about the Church, all of which separate Ins and Outs with $p < .0001$ and have either an In or Out mean score beyond the $+2$ ("Probably") point. All of these beliefs are of the "God and the Other World" type, appearing to discriminate better because no pool of evidence common to Ins and Outs relates to them. The most important items are the two that lie near the core of the In belief complex: "Christ rose from the dead" and "Christ is really present in the Eucharist." The interpretation of a figure who lived two milennia ago is a major touchstone separating these one hundred Ins and Outs. It is difficult not to think of the words of this figure in the Gospel, "Who do you say that I am?"[3]

3. Matthew 16:15. See Chapter 10 of this study for follow-up information on these two beliefs.

FIVE

What They Value

One way of conceptualizing this study is to say it is the search for a line, for some border between Ins and Outs that is not shown in one's immediate perception of them. Such a line was found in the beliefs of Ins and Outs about points of Catholic doctrine, though the line was clearer for one kind of belief than for another. In the present chapter, we seek to uncover a line in the things these people value, the things they say are important to them.

At the outset it was thought that Ins and Outs might simply value different things, Outs, for example, putting a greater premium on change, open-mindedness, and freedom, Ins thinking more of loyalty to one's background and stability in one's philosophy of life. Yet these differences were not expected to be great—indeed, one reason for being so curious about the border between Ins and Outs in the first place was that they seemed to be quite similar in the things they valued.

If they were alike in *what* they valued, one important difference between them might be in their perception of how the Catholic Church affected their values, that is, in how *instrumental* they perceived membership to be in attaining them. Ins and Outs might both value changing one's outlook on life;

Outs might see membership in the Catholic Church as blocking the attainment of that goal, whereas Ins might see membership as aiding it. Both Ins and Outs might value open-mindedness, the Outs thinking that being open-minded was impossible in the Church and the Ins thinking the opposite.

One way of mapping attitudes, that described by Milton J. Rosenberg (1956, 1960) in connection with his affective-cognitive consistency model of attitude change, seemed particularly suited to the questions these speculations raised. A diagram of that model adapted to the present investigation appears in Figure 5.1. To assess a subject's value system with respect to the Church, we ask him to rate the importance of each of twenty values on a nine-point scale and then to rate on a five-point scale whether membership in the Church helps or hinders the attainment of each value. In-Out differences in the former would indicate that these two groups of people value different things. Differences in the latter would mean that they have different perceptions about the instrumentality of membership in fulfilling each value.

Simple mathematical operations can then be performed on each subject's data. Each item's Value score can be multiplied by its Instrumentality score to indicate whether membership in the Church hinders or helps the attainment of values important to the subject. Using these Value-Instrumentality scores, one can point to critical areas of difference between Ins and Outs, areas in which Ins think membership is especially fulfilling and Outs think it is especially abrasive.

The twenty Value-Instrumentality scores can then be summed for each subject. This Value-Instrumentality Sum tells us how positive or negative the subject feels toward membership in the Church, taking all the values into consideration. Naturally, we would expect a positive score for Ins and a negative one for Outs.

Finally, extending Rosenberg's procedure, we can devise a measure of the ambivalence felt by a person toward member-

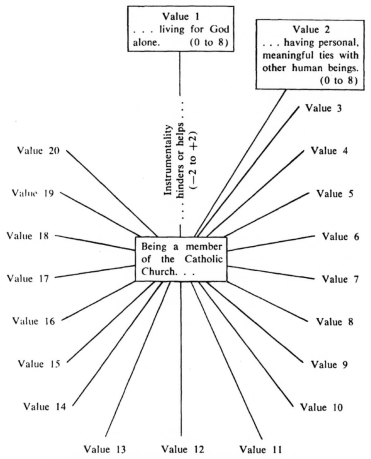

Value 1
. . . living for God
alone.   (0 to 8)

Value 2
. . . having personal,
meaningful ties with
other human beings.
            (0 to 8)

Value 3

Value 4

Value 5

Value 6

Value 7

Value 8

Value 9

Value 10

Value 20

Value 19

Value 18

Value 17

Value 16

Value 15

Value 14

Being a member
of the Catholic
Church. . .

Instrumentality
. . . hinders or helps . . .
(−2 to +2)

Value 13   Value 12   Value 11

V: Subject rates 20 values on a 0 to 8 scale.

I: Subject rates instrumentality of membership in attaining each value on a −2 to +2 scale.

VI: Value scores are multiplied by Instrumentality scores to indicate whether membership hinders (−) or helps (+) in attaining values important to the subject.

ΣVI: Value-Instrumentality scores are summed to indicate how positive or negative subject is toward membership in the Church.

Σ|VI| − |ΣVI|: Absolute Value-Instrumentality Sum is subtracted from the sum of the absolute Value-Instrumentality scores to indicate how ambivalent subject is toward membership in the Church.

Figure 5.1. A model for assessing values and the role of Church membership in attaining those values (after Rosenberg, 1956, 1960).

ship in the Church. The basic idea is simple: ambivalence in the present context means that with respect to the first value, membership looks attractive to a person, with respect to the second, it looks unattractive, with respect to the third, it again looks attractive, and so on. A person with ten positive and ten negative Value-Instrumentality scores would be highly ambivalent toward membership, whereas a person with all twenty scores positive or all twenty negative would not be ambivalent at all. An overall ambivalence score can be determined by subtracting the absolute Value-Instrumentality Sum from the sum of the absolute Value-Instrumentality scores (see Figure 5.1). This measure of ambivalence will be of use later on when the search for why is begun: one hypothesis for why people leave the Church is that they cannot tolerate the ambiguity membership presents. On this basis, we would expect Outs to show less ambivalence toward membership than Ins.

The Importance of Twenty Values

Figure 5.2 and Table 5.1 list the twenty values presented to subjects, arranged according to the degree to which they distinguish Ins from Outs. Three of these items were written to express a desire for *Religious fulfillment* (e.g., "Living for God alone"); these values, it should be noted, are belief-tied, i.e., whether one accepts them as values will depend in part on what he believes about God, Christ, and sin. Three more items were intended to express a *General* desire for *human fulfillment* (e.g., "Having personal, meaningful ties with other human beings"). Two items were meant to determine whether a subject valued *Stability* in his outlook on life and two, by contrast, whether he valued *Change* (e.g., "Having a stable philosophy of life" versus "Having my beliefs, values, and assumptions shaken up from time to time"). Two expressed a desire for *Authority* and two a desire for *Freedom* ("Having dependable people in authority to rely on" versus "Being able to think and act for myself"), one of the authority items also involving the notion of religious fulfillment. Six other items expressed a variety of things subjects might attach importance to.

Figure 5.2 reveals that the values that best discriminate Ins and Outs are the belief-tied items expressing a desire for religious fulfillment. They are, in general, of no importance to Outs and moderately important to Ins. Items having to do

Table 5.1. In-Out Differences in the Acceptance of Twenty Values

Value No. and Type		Mean Ins	Mean Outs	Mean In-Out Diff.	F	p<
11	Religious fulfillment	4.92	1.30	3.62	80.30	.0001
17	Authority/Religious fulfillment	4.52	1.22	3.30	64.82	.0001
1	Religious fulfillment	3.44	.64	2.80	37.14	.0001
19	Religious fulfillment	2.30	.50	1.80	36.76	.0001
8	Freedom	5.76	6.86	−1.10	19.81	.0001
16	Freedom	4.36	5.74	−1.38	15.22	.0002
13	Change-Openness	1.42	2.74	−1.32	10.06	.0021
20	General human fulfillment	3.84	4.96	−1.12	9.27	.0031
9	Other	5.34	6.08	− .74	8.37	.0048
15	Other	3.96	4.78	− .82	6.56	.0120
5	Change-Openness	3.64	4.28	− .64	2.75	.1007
14	Stability-Closedness	1.46	.98	.48	1.67	.1995
10	General human fulfillment	6.38	6.78	− .40	1.45	.2318
12	Other	4.58	4.92	− .34	1.03	.3121
6	Other	4.18	3.98	.20	.31	.5820
18	Other	4.84	4.68	.16	.18	.6735
3	Other	6.06	5.98	.08	.06	.8069
2	General human fulfillment	6.74	6.68	.06	.06	.8145
4	Stability-Closedness	4.32	4.24	.08	.04	.8513
7	Authority	2.08	2.08	.00	.00	1.000
Average of 20 items		4.21	3.97	.24	2.56	.1128

Note: Items are arranged in order of *F* values, which indicate the degree to which the distribution of In scores is different from the distribution of Out scores. For the full wording of each item, see Figure 5.2.

Figure 5.2. In-Out differences in the acceptance of twenty values. The bar represents the size of the mean In-Out difference. Items are arranged in order of F values (see Table 5.1). See Appendix II, p. 226 for the full wording of the scale points.

Type		Not Important in My Life 0	Only as Important as 15 or 20 Other Things 2	Only One of 7 or 8 Important Things 4	One of the 3 Most Important Things 6	The Most Important Thing in My Life 8
Religious fulfillment	11. Spreading the message of Christ.	Outs ▬▬▬▬▬ Ins				
Authority/Religious fulfillment	17. Following the precepts of God in my moral actions.	Outs ▬▬▬▬▬ Ins				
Religious fulfillment	1. Living for God alone.	Outs ▬▬▬▬▬▬▬▬ Ins				
Religious fulfillment	19. Atoning for my sins.	Outs ▬▬▬▬▬▬▬ Ins				
Freedom	8. Being able to think and act for myself.			Ins ▭▭ Outs		
Freedom	16. Being able to determine my own code of morality.				Ins ▭▭ Outs	
Change-Openness	13. Escaping the confines of my early background.		Ins ▭▭▭▭▭ Outs			
General human fulfillment	20. Being able to live with some of my inadequacies.			Ins ▭▭ Outs		
Other	9. Having interesting and worthwhile work to do.				Ins ▭▭ Outs	

Category	Item	Scale
Other	15. Having a satisfactory sexual outlet.	Ins☐ Outs
Change-Openness	5. Having my beliefs, values, and assumptions shaken up from time to time.	Ins☐ Outs
Stability-Closedness	14. Remaining loyal to the truths I was taught while growing up.	Outs■ Ins
General human fulfillment	10. Becoming a full human being.	Ins☐ Outs
Other	12. Accomplishing something for the underprivileged, the poverty-stricken.	Ins☐ Outs
Other	6. Making a significant contribution in the intellectual community.	Outs■ Ins
Other	18. Accomplishing something for the cause of world peace.	Outs■ Ins
Other	3. Being happily married and having a family.	Outs■ Ins
General human fulfillment	2. Having personal, meaningful ties with other human beings.	Outs■ Ins
Stability-Closedness	4. Having a stable philosophy of life.	Outs■ Ins
Authority	7. Having dependable people in authority to rely on.	Outs Ins
	Average of 20 items	Outs■ Ins

with human fulfillment, in general, do not distinguish well between Ins and Outs, both groups placing a high premium on them. While Outs see religious fulfillment as incompatible with human fulfillment, Ins feel that having religious values does not detract from fulfilling oneself as a human being. "Living for God alone" and "Having personal, meaningful ties with other human beings" is more a contradiction for Outs than for Ins.

Freedom to think for oneself and to determine one's own code of morality are rated as more important by Outs than by Ins, though one *Authority* item meant to contrast with the *Freedom* items shows no In-Out difference. The other *Authority* item shows a large difference, but it involves the notion of religious fulfillment. In the same vein as above, "Following the precepts of God in my moral actions" and "Being able to determine my own code of morality" are seen as compatible by Ins and incompatible by Outs.

Outs are slightly more desirous of change in their outlook on life, but both Ins and Outs are alike in subscribing to values expressing stability. Both change and stability are moderately desirable to both groups. The slightly higher rating given by Outs to the *Change* values may be as much a result of their present status as a cause of it, but we cannot be certain.

Of the six mixed items, two that discriminate between Ins and Outs are "having interesting and worthwhile work to do" and "having a satisfactory sexual outlet," both of which are given slightly higher ratings by Outs.

In general, Ins and Outs are quite alike in the things they say they value. The correlation between the order in which the Ins subscribe to the twenty values and the order in which the Outs do is $+.734$ ($p < .01$, 1-tailed). On the average, a value item is given a 4.21 rating by Ins and a 3.97 rating by Outs, Ins being more positive on eleven items and Outs on nine. The five items rated highest by each group are identical, though ordered in a slightly different way:

Having personal, meaningful ties with other human beings. (Average: 6.71; Ins: 6.74; Outs: 6.68)

Becoming a full human being. (Average: 6.58; Ins: 6.38; Outs: 6.78)

Being able to think and act for myself. (Average: 6.31; Ins: 5.76; Outs: 6.86)

Being happily married and having a family. (Average: 6.02; Ins: 6.06; Outs: 5.98)

Having interesting and worthwhile work to do. (Average: 5.71; Ins: 5.34; Outs: 6.08)

The major point of difference is that Ins consider religious fulfillment moderately important and Outs consider it of no importance.

This conclusion is substantiated by open-ended questions asked prior to the presentation of the list of values.[1] Asked what they would like to accomplish in life, whom they admired, what causes they would like to see succeed and what causes fail, Ins and Outs gave surprisingly similar answers. The only significant difference that emerged from their coded replies is that a few Ins (six) mentioned religious fulfillment as among those things they most wished to accomplish, while no Outs did so.

Because Ins and Outs are close in their assessment of other values, it seems that religious values can be added to or taken away from their value systems with little effect elsewhere. The religious values of the Ins appear to be something over and above their other values. They do not seem to cause value changes in nonreligious areas.

1. See Appendix II, p. 227, Questions 1–5. Coding on Question 2 was not needed and on Question 3 it proved impossible. Agreement between two judges on Question 1 was 92.5 per cent and on Questions 4 and 5 it was 90 per cent. Cases disagreed upon were placed in "Other."

Instrumentality of Membership

The differences between Ins and Outs become more significant when they are asked to rate how membership in the Church affects the attainment of each of the twenty values. In thinking about the results from this part of the questionnaire, we should keep in mind that each subject rated how

Table 5.2. In-Out Differences in Twenty Instrumentality-of-Membership Ratings

Value No. and Type		Mean Ins	Mean Outs	Mean In-Out Diff.	F	p<
10	General human fulfillment	1.44	− .80	2.24	159.80	.0001
2	General human fulfillment	1.44	− .12	1.56	78.25	.0001
8	Freedom	−.14	−1.62	1.48	52.95	.0001
18	Other	1.16	.00	1.16	50.52	.0001
16	Freedom	−.22	−1.66	1.44	49.22	.0001
3	Other	1.20	.00	1.20	39.28	.0001
13	Change-Openness	−.46	−1.54	1.08	36.76	.0001
12	Other	1.22	.24	.98	32.97	.0001
5	Change-Openness	.06	−1.28	1.34	32.30	.0001
20	General human fulfillment	1.10	− .10	1.20	29.96	.0001
6	Other	.16	− .58	.74	16.94	.0001
15	Other	−.10	− .82	.72	12.65	.0006
7	Authority	.12	.74	−.62	7.10	.0091
9	Other	.40	.10	.30	5.66	.0194
11	Religious fulfillment	1.54	1.12	.42	4.17	.0439
1	Religious fulfillment	1.46	1.08	.38	3.00	.0864
14	Stability-Closedness fulfillment	1.02	1.40	−.38	2.94	.0899
17	Authority/Religious	1.12	.92	.30	.85	.3581
19	Religious fulfillment	1.26	1.18	.08	.20	.6589
4	Stability-Closedness	.82	.80	.02	.01	.9291
Average of 20 items		.73	− .05	.78	72.81	.0001

Note: Items are arranged in order of *F* values, which indicate the degree to which the distribution of In scores is different from the distribution of Out scores. For the full wording of each item, see Figure 5.3.

membership affected or would affect his own fulfillment of a particular value (as opposed to that of people in general).

The largest discrepancies between Ins and Outs (see Figure 5.3 and Table 5.2) have to do with the role of membership in enabling one to fulfill himself as a human being, Ins thinking of membership as quite helpful and Outs saying it would be of no help or even a slight hindrance. Outs see membership as a definite hindrance to freedom and change, and Ins see it as basically indifferent. Interestingly enough, Ins see membership as a help to a number of mixed values ("something for world peace," "happily married," "something for the underprivileged"), while Outs say membership would do little to help or hinder them in achieving these goals. If one is a member, it seems the positive effects of membership are seen as far-reaching.

Ins see membership as more helpful than Outs on eighteen of the values, while Outs see it as more helpful on two (both of which are of little importance to Ins or Outs). Averaging across all items, Ins see membership as .73 scale points more helpful than Outs. The correlation between In and Out rank-orders of these twenty Instrumentality items is +.618 ($p <$ .01, 1-tailed), meaning that each item tends to evoke a similar response from each group, once the major In-Out difference is allowed for.

Value-Instrumentality Scores

The assessment described in the previous section took no account of the importance of the value that membership was seen as helping or hindering. Differences in the perception of the instrumentality of membership would be of no consequence unless the value involved were an important one. Multiplying the Value score of each item by its Instrumentality score and comparing Ins and Outs on the distributions of scores that result will tell us where membership is perceived differently with

Figure 5.3. In-Out differences in twenty instrumentality-of-membership ratings. The bar represents the size of the mean In-Out difference. Items are arranged in order of F values (see Table 5.2).

Type	Being a member of the Catholic Church...	Hinders −2	Slightly Hinders −1	Neither Helps Nor Hinders 0	Slightly Helps +1	Helps +2	
General human fulfillment	Being a member of the Catholic Church...		Outs			Ins	...becoming a full human being. (10)
General human fulfillment	Being a member of the Catholic Church...			Outs		Ins	...having personal, meaningful ties with other human beings. (2)
Freedom	Being a member of the Catholic Church...	Outs		Ins			...being able to think and act for myself. (8)
Other	Being a member of the Catholic Church...			Outs	Ins		...accomplishing something for the cause of world peace. (18)
Freedom	Being a member of the Catholic Church...	Outs		Ins			...being able to determine my own code of morality. (16)
Other	Being a member of the Catholic Church...			Outs		Ins	...being happily married and having a family. (3)
Change-Openness	Being a member of the Catholic Church...	Outs		Ins			...escaping the confines of my early background. (13)
Other	Being a member of the Catholic Church...			Outs		Ins	...accomplishing something for the underprivileged, the poverty-stricken. (12)
Change-Openness	Being a member of the Catholic Church...		Outs	Ins			...having my beliefs, values, and assumptions shaken up from time to time. (5)

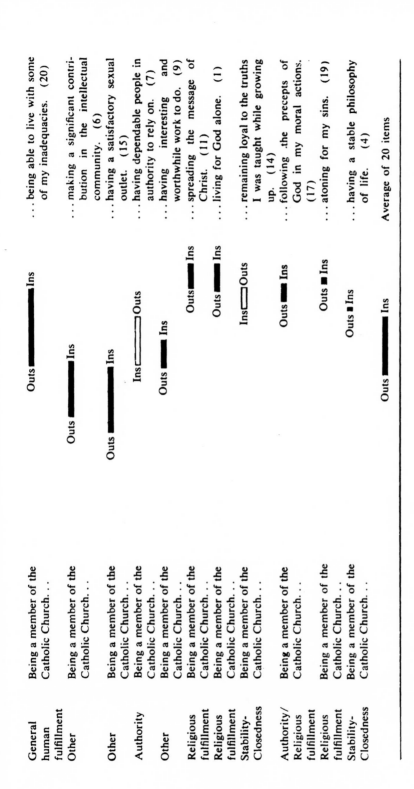

respect to values that are important. Table 5.3 lists the twenty items again, this time arranging them according to the degree to which their Value-Instrumentality scores distinguish Ins and Outs.

Table 5.3. In-Out Differences in Twenty Value-Instrumentality Scores

Value No. and Type	Mean Ins	Mean Outs	Mean In-Out Diff.	F	p <
10 General human fulfillment	9.60	− 5.44	15.04	141.35	.0001
2 General human fulfillment	9.76	− .90	10.66	74.84	.0001
16 Freedom	−.22	− 9.34	9.12	69.34	.0001
11 Religious fulfillment	7.78	.48	7.30	64.57	.0001
8 Freedom	−.44	−10.98	10.54	63.60	.0001
18 Other	5.82	− .22	6.04	41.61	.0001
1 Religious fulfillment	5.62	.42	5.20	37.42	.0001
13 Change-Openness	−.02	− 4.86	4.84	37.35	.0001
5 Change-Openness	.78	− 5.44	6.22	33.58	.0001
3 Other	7.22	.10	7.12	32.73	.0001
17 Authority/Religious fulfillment	5.42	.88	4.54	27.29	.0001
19 Religious fulfillment	3.14	.46	2.68	21.28	.0001
12 Other	5.80	1.24	4.56	20.66	.0001
20 General human fulfillment	4.12	− .50	4.62	17.34	.0001
6 Other	1.02	− 2.24	3.26	14.38	.0003
15 Other	−.42	− 3.52	3.10	10.88	.0014
14 Stability-Closedness	2.12	.76	1.36	5.07	.0266
9 Other	2.08	.56	1.52	4.22	.0427
7 Authority	−.18	.94	−1.12	3.85	.0528
4 Stability-Closedness	3.88	2.84	1.04	.79	.3751
Average of 20 items	3.64	− 1.61	5.25	123.97	.0001

Note: Items are arranged in order of F values, which indicate the degree to which the distribution of In scores is different from the distribution of Out scores. The Value-Instrumentality scores reveal the extent to which the Church hinders (−) or helps (+) the attainment of values important to the subject.

The best discriminants again have to do with general human fulfillment, which is valued highly by both Ins and Outs. Ins, however, see membership in the Church as a positive means to fulfillment and Outs see it either as an obstacle to fulfillment or as indifferent to fulfillment. Freedom is likewise valued by both Ins and Outs, but Outs see membership as a hindrance to freedom while Ins say membership is indifferent to freedom. Finally, both Ins and Outs agree that membership in the Church would aid in "spreading the message of Christ"; however, this is a value only for Ins, not for Outs.

Figures 5.4 and 5.5 are simplified diagrams of the typical value systems of Ins and Outs, showing whether each of the five items at the top of Table 5.3 is valued by subjects and whether membership in the Church is seen as instrumental in attaining the value. These diagrams highlight the major differences in the two value systems.

Although one shies away from language implying causality at this stage of the analysis, if we were asked to look at the diagrams and say why Ins are in and Outs are out, we could reply that, with respect to these values, Ins remain members because the Church helps them become more fully human, helps them establish ties with other human beings, helps them spread the message of Christ, and is not an obstacle to their strong desire for freedom of thought and action. Outs are no longer members because the Church is a definite hindrance to freedom of thought and action, because it is a hindrance to becoming fully human, because it does nothing to help them establish ties with others, and because it fosters something they care nothing about.

As expected, the ΣVI scores, indicating overall positive or negative feeling toward membership in the Church, are greatly different for Ins and Outs ($+72.88$ mean In score versus -32.22 mean Out score; $F = 123.97$; $p < .001$; in the simplified diagrams, the In ΣVI score is $+3$ and the Out ΣVI score

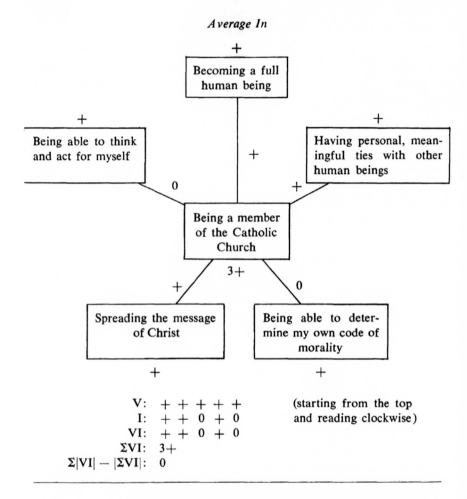

$$V: \quad + + + + +$$
$$I: \quad + + \ 0 + 0$$
$$VI: \quad + + \ 0 + 0$$
$$\Sigma VI: \quad 3+$$
$$\Sigma|VI| - |\Sigma VI|: \quad 0$$

Figure 5.4. Simplified diagram of Ins' value system with re-
spect to the Church. Those values whose Value-
Instrumentality scores best distinguish Ins and
Outs were used.

Value: + *if above 4.0*   Instrumentality: + *if above +.5*
    0 *if below 1.5*   0 *if +.5 to −.5*
                                              − *if below −.5*

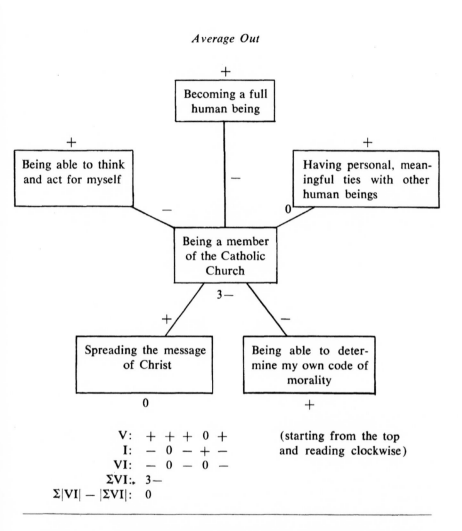

Figure 5.5. Simplified diagrams of Outs' value system with respect to the Church. Those values whose Value-Instrumentality scores best distinguish Ins and Outs were used. The signs were determined as in Figure 5.4.

is -3). Contrary to one hypothesis, Ins showed slightly less ambivalence ($\Sigma|VI| - |\Sigma VI|$ score) in their acceptance of membership than Outs did in their rejection of it (24.84 mean In score versus 35.72 mean Out score; $F = 4.15$, $p < .0445$; in the simplified diagrams, both ambivalence scores are zero).

Summary

It was asked at the outset of this chapter whether Ins and Outs value different things or, valuing similar things, see differently the relationship of membership to these values. Figures 5.4 and 5.5 indicate that only one of the five best In-Out discriminants results from acceptance of different values, whereas four out of five result from differing perceptions of the instrumentality links between membership and the values. Ten out of the twenty Value items show statistically significant differences, whereas fifteen of the twenty Instrumentality items and eighteen of the twenty Value-Instrumentality items do. It seems that greater differences come out when perceptions of what the Catholic Church is are brought into play.

SIX

The Two Churches

What was intimated in the previous chapter becomes manifest in the present: the Church that the Ins are in is not the Church that the Outs are out of. To understand this statement more precisely we must look at replies to the questions contained in that part of the interview entitled "Definition of the Church." The discussion of these results will center around four major areas: (1) subjects' general definition and perception of the Church, (2) their perception of what the Church believes, (3) their perception of the change in the Church, and (4) their perception of the criteria of membership in the Church.

General Definition and Perception of the Church

The section of the questionnaire to be discussed here began with the simple question: "How would you *define* the Catholic Church?" While it produced no replies that could be conveniently categorized, it did provide insight into the ways individuals thought about the Church. The basic thrust of their remarks was picked up in quantified form later in the interview as subjects answered more formally structured questions about the Church.

Open-ended definitions of the Church typically given by
Outs included:

> a hierarchy of rulers setting certain standards of living
>
> an organized religion whose goal is to make everyone
> Catholic
>
> an institution geared toward forcing people to live holy
> lives by imposing restrictions on them
>
> an institution whose basic tenets are belief in Christ
> and adherence to certain laws that have developed
> within the Church and that are morally binding on
> members
>
> a political hierarchy proposing and enforcing a definite
> set of morals and dogma
>
> an institution run from Rome by the pope and cardi-
> nals

On occasion, Out definitions pointed to hollowness, self-
interest, or hypocrisy on the part of the Church:

> a highly structured organization that has taken an es-
> sentially humanistic message and turned it into a re-
> ligiously vested interest
>
> an institution whose function is to mass market its
> conception of Christianity and perpetuate its own ex-
> istence
>
> an organized religion, rich and powerful and cynical
>
> an ancient institution closely bound with the cultural
> history of the West that has on its conscience its ina-
> bility to promote justice and moral responsibility in the
> people under its control

a social institution nominally committed to promotion of Christian values but in practice more concerned with maintenance of its own position

an institutional organization that pretends to practice the teachings of Jesus Christ and sets up guidelines to direct men's lives

Definitions provided by Ins, in contrast, either omitted the notion of organization/institution or assigned it secondary importance. Usually, Ins spoke of a body or community of people and included some reference to the divine:

a body of men united under a common belief seeking the perfection of themselves and the world

a body of believers worshipping God through Christ as God Incarnate and attempting to carry out in the world the teachings of Christ through a hierarchical and sacramental structure

the membership organized to formulate their worship, their responsibility to one another and to those outside the Church

a group of people in Evanston that I worship with, but with a sense of being in community with a larger body of people

a group of individuals concerned with God as seen in their fellow men

a group of people who recognize some sort of ultimate reality, who recognize that Christ was speaking truth about this ultimate reality, and who realize that man needs to live in community

the people of God

the Mystical Body of Christ

the body of all baptized persons who follow Catholic beliefs, guided by the spirit of God

Six Ins (and no Outs) portrayed a Church that encompassed those not ordinarily thought of as Catholic. Some of their definitions were:

the universal Church of all men, the community of all men

anyone who, in his thinking and living, carries out the ideals of Christ, whether he realizes it or not (so an atheist could be in the Church)

a starting point for involving oneself in causes of brotherhood, understanding, peace

Nine Ins (and four Outs) split the Church into several aspects or "Churches," there generally being two, one the institutional Church identified with the hierarchy and the other the grass-roots Church of the members. Indeed, some Ins found it so difficult to speak of the Church as a single entity that the questions I posed had to be answered separately for each Church. On occasion, I found myself asking whether they were speaking of "Church Number One" or "Church Number Two" and writing their replies in pencil for one Church and ink for the other. All but one of these Ins, however, said they belonged to both aspects or "Churches," though they were closer to the grass-roots Church of the members.

Figure 6.1 and Table 6.1 list the mean In-Out differences in response to scaled questionnaire items covering subjects' general definition and perception of the Church. All the items but the last are highly significant discriminants. Ins incorporate both human and divine, visible and invisible elements into their definition of the Church, whereas Outs say the Church is simply a visible human institution. This disparity corroborates the general impressions noted above of subjects' open-ended definitions of the Church.

Looked at more concretely, the Church delineated by the Ins is more a community of individuals than the one described by the Outs. The Ins' Church is also more flexible, more liberal, less dogmatic, less monolithic, and less a controller of people's consciences. Further substantiation of these discrepancies in perception comes from subjects' ratings of what the Church thinks it should do in the future. Ins perceive the Church as significantly more liberal in this regard: they say the Church is more willing to phase out the parochial school system, to place laymen on the boards of trustees of Catholic colleges, to pursue the ecumenical movement, and is less insistent on bringing all people "into the fold." [1]

Table 6.1. In-Out Differences in the Perception of the Catholic Church

Description of Church	Mean Ins	Mean Outs	Mean In-Out Diff.	F	p <
Human	2.92	4.66	−1.74	40.84	.0001
Invisible	2.44	1.56	.88	9.55	.0027
Free consciences	2.78	1.34	1.44	29.78	.0001
A community of individuals	2.74	1.36	1.38	28.52	.0001
Flexible	2.84	1.56	1.28	21.25	.0001
Liberal	2.26	1.22	1.04	20.32	.0001
Pass down dogma	3.04	4.16	−1.12	15.66	.0002
One school of thought	1.94	3.16	−1.22	15.32	.0002
Directed to the next world	2.84	3.22	−.38	1.62	.2057

Note: Items are arranged in order of *F* values, which indicate the degree to which the distribution of In scores is different from the distribution of Out scores. See Figure 6.1, and see Appendix II.

1. See Appendix II, pp. 235–236, items 21–26. The four differences reported here are significant with $p < .03$ (*t* test, 2-tailed).

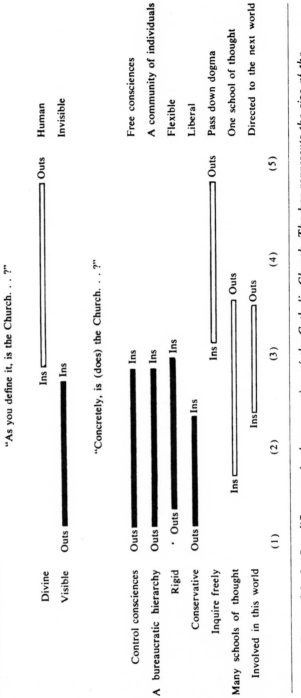

Figure 6.1. *In-Out differences in the perception of the Catholic Church. The bar represents the size of the mean In-Out difference. Items are arranged in order of F values (see Table 6.1). For the full wording of each item, see Appendix II, pp. 245–246, Questions 2, 3, 6–12.*

Even with the above differences, however, both Ins and Outs view the Church on the bureaucratic, rigid, conservative, dogmatic and controlling side. The one exception to this pattern is that Ins recognize many schools of thought in the Church and Outs see at least more than one. The Catholic Church appears monolithic to neither group.

Table 6.2 likewise confirms general impressions received from subjects' open-ended definitions of the Church. When asked, "Who is the Catholic Church?," the large majority of Ins said "the people" and very few even mentioned the hierarchy or the clergy. The Outs nearly reversed this, the majority including the hierarchy/clergy in their conception of the Catholic Church and less than a third saying it was the people alone. The core of the Church, to Ins, was either the people or God, while to Outs it was the hierarchy/clergy. Both Ins and Outs located the people at the periphery, though when asked this question a number of Ins balked at a core-periphery distinction. In all, eleven Ins, as compared with thirty-seven Outs, said the hierarchy or the clergy was more central than the people. A number of Ins and only one Out said that one's position near the center of the Church depended upon internal characteristics such as one's degree of commitment to the Church or one's involvement in the Church's change.

Ins and Outs were not as discrepant when asked to identify the locus of power in the Church (Table 6.3). They differed in response to the simple question, "Where is the power in the Catholic Church?," about half the Ins but nearly all the Outs saying it rested with the hierarchy/clergy alone. But they were close to agreeing that the hierarchy/clergy have the most power and they agreed that the people have the least power. There is no significant difference between the two groups in making an overall distinction in the locus of power.

The Church of the Ins, then, may be described as a community of people who are the real center of the Church and a clerical hierarchy who have most of the power in the Church.

Table 6.2. In-Out Differences in the Perception of the Core and Periphery of the Catholic Church

"Who is the Catholic Church?"	Ins (N)	Outs (N)	χ^2, df, p
(1) The people	37	15	
(2) The people and the hierarchy/clergy	3	13	$\chi^2 = 30.92$
(3) The hierarchy/clergy	1	17	$df = 3$
(4) Other	9	5	$p < .001$
"Who is at its core?"			
(1) The people	17	4	
(2) The people and the hierarchy/clergy	2	5	
(3) The hierarchy/clergy	8	35	$\chi^2 = 36.25$
(4) Jesus Christ, God, Holy Spirit	19	5	$df = 4$
(5) Other	4	1	$p < .001$
"Who is at its periphery?"			
(1) The people	33	39	
(2) The people and the hierarchy/clergy	0	5	
(3) The hierarchy/clergy	1	2	
(4) No one, or "core-periphery" distinction			$\chi^2 = 17.30$
not made	14	1	$df = 4$
(5) Other	2	3	$p < .005$
The core-periphery distinction			
(1) Hierarchy/clergy more central than			
people	11	37	
(2) People more central than or at same			
level as hierarchy/clergy	5	7	
(3) Distinction based on internal charac-			
teristics of individuals	16	1	$\chi^2 = 35.00$
(hierarchy/clergy not mentioned)			$df = 3$
(4) No distinction made	18	5	$p < .001$

Note: Answers to the four questions involved (see Appendix II, p. 246, Questions 13–15) were coded independently and blindly by two judges into nine categories. The judges agreed 92 per cent of the time; cases disagreed upon were placed into a more inclusive category or "other." The above categories are those of the original nine with the highest frequencies of response, the other categories being collapsed into "Other." *People* included "the people of God," "all the members," "laity," "me." *Hierarchy/clergy* included "pope," "Curia," "Vatican," "bishops," "priests," "nuns." *Internal characteristics* included "closeness to God," "commitment to Church," "involvement in change."

Table 6.3. In-Out Differences in the Perception of the Locus of Power in the Catholic Church

"Where is the power (in general) in the Catholic Church?"	Ins (N)	Outs (N)	χ^2, df, p
(1) The people	7	1	
(2) The people and the hierarchy/clergy	10	2	$\chi^2 = 16.06$
(3) The hierarchy/clergy	26	44	$df = 3$
(4) Other	7	3	$p < .005$
"Who has the most power?"			
(1) The people	5	1	
(2) The people and the hierarchy/clergy	6	1	$\chi^2 = 9.32$
(3) The hierarchy/clergy	34	46	$df = 3$
(4) Other	5	2	$p < .03$
"Who has the least power?"			
(1) The people	37	38	
(2) The people and the hierarchy/clergy	1	4	$\chi^2 = 3.81$
(3) The hierarchy/clergy	6	6	$df = 3$
(4) Other	6	2	N.S.
The most-least power distinction			
(1) Hierarchy/clergy has more power than people	35	42	
(2) People have more power or as much power as hierarchy/clergy	7	2	$\chi^2 = 3.71$ $df = 2$
(3) Other, including no distinction made	8	6	N.S.

Note: See Appendix II, p. 247, Questions 17–20. Coding procedure was identical with that described in Table 6.2, the judges agreeing 97 per cent of the time.

The Church of the Outs is simply the all powerful clerical hierarchy, the "institutional" or "organizational" Church. In addition, the Church of the Ins contains an element of the divine, described variously as God, Jesus Christ, or the Holy Spirit. It is more liberal and flexible, less dogmatic, controlling and monolithic than that of the Outs.

In and Out definitions and perceptions of the Church are not generated in a vacuum. There are in Catholic literary circles, and in the mass media as well, a number of theologians —bishops, priests, and laymen—who probably serve as models for these definitions and perceptions of the Church, especially in the case of Ins. Much of what was said by Ins and Outs about the Church can also be found in the writings of these theologians and in the work of priests who are dissociated in one way or another from the church.[2]

Perception of What the Church Believes

After subjects stated whether *they* agreed or disagreed with twenty belief-formulas (Figure 4.1), they were told to "go through these statements a second time and indicate what you believe is the *thinking of the Church*—as you define the Church—on these matters." Their perception of what the Church believes regarding these items is shown in Figure 6.2 and Table 6.4. In every case, the Outs see the Church as more orthodox than do Ins. In thirteen instances the In-Out difference in perception attains statistical significance ($p < .05$). The average difference for twenty items is significant at the .0001 level.

Laws of cognitive consistency are clearly at work in determining the relationship between what one believes and what he thinks the Church believes. Figure 6.3 (III) depicts the average In and the average Out beliefs (S) and the average In and the average Out perception of what the Church believes (C). Ins, being associated with the Church (+), bring their beliefs more in line with the Church's and also bring the Church's beliefs more in line with their own. Outs, being dissociated from the Church (−), do the opposite: the spread between themselves and the Church is greatly inflated.

2. See works by Baum, Callahan, Davis, Greeley, Kavanaugh, Kung, McKenzie, Ruether, and Suenens listed in the bibliography. See also *Time* magazine article by Henderson.

In approaching congruity between what he believes and what he perceives to be the thinking of the Church, the In on some occasions feels the Church pulling him and on others finds himself pulling the Church. Apparently there are some beliefs, most notably "Christ rose from the dead" (Figure 6.3 (I), Item 5), that the In realizes the Church will not compromise on. Since these beliefs are ambiguous enough (see Chapter 4) to permit movement by the subject, he finds himself

Table 6.4. In-Out Differences in the Perception of "the Thinking of the Church" on Twenty Beliefs

Belief No. and Type	Mean Ins	Mean Outs	Mean In-Out Diff.	F	p <
16 Morality	.90	2.40	−1.50	26.99	.0001
14 Man	1.00	2.24	−1.24	19.55	.0001
17 Mary	1.80	2.62	− .82	11.59	.0010
8 Morality	.92	2.02	−1.10	11.07	.0013
11 Church	1.90	2.72	− .82	11.06	.0013
7 Mary	2.02	2.66	− .64	10.19	.0020
4 Morality	1.40	2.30	− .90	9.85	.0023
12 Morality	1.94	2.60	− .66	8.84	.0038
1 Church	1.84	2.58	− .74	6.97	.0097
18 Man	2.34	2.78	− .44	6.86	.0103
20 Morality	.74	1.62	− .88	6.79	.0107
2 Man	.96	1.80	− .84	6.49	.0125
19 Afterlife	2.12	2.62	− .50	5.20	.0248
13 God	2.60	2.88	− .28	3.45	.0664
15 Christ	2.72	2.90	− .18	2.83	.0961
9 Afterlife	2.56	2.84	− .28	2.81	.0972
6 Man	2.74	2.92	− .18	1.92	.1694
10 Man	2.60	2.78	− .18	1.73	.1913
3 God	2.88	2.92	− .04	.15	.7012
5 Christ	2.90	2.92	− .02	.07	.7893
Average of 20 items	1.94	2.56	− .62	17.20	.0001

Note: Items are arranged in order of *F* values, which indicate the degree to which the distribution of In scores is different from the distribution of Out scores. For the full wording of each item, see Figure 6.2.

Type		No Position One Way or the Other 0	Possibly True +1	Probably True +2	Definitely True +3
Morality	16. There is an objective moral law valid for all men of all times.		Ins ========= Outs		
Man	14. People can be divided into two distinct classes: those in the state of grace and those not in the state of grace.		Ins ========= Outs		
Mary	17. Mary's body was assumed into heaven.			Ins ======== Outs	
Morality	8. Deliberately missing Mass on Sunday is a mortal sin.		Ins ============= Outs		
Church	11. The pope is infallible when speaking on matters of faith and morals.			Ins ========== Outs	
Mary	7. In conceiving and giving birth to Our Lord, Mary retained her virginity.			Ins ====== Outs	
Morality	4. Premarital sexual intercourse is morally wrong.			Ins ======= Outs	
Morality	12. Abortion is morally wrong.			Ins ======== Outs	

Category	Item	Scale
Church	1. The Catholic Church is the one true Church.	Ins ⬜ Outs
Man	18. Every man is born with original sin.	Ins ⬜ Outs
Morality	20. The use of artificial contraceptives is morally wrong.	Ins ⬜ Outs
Man	2. Mortification of the flesh is essential to human perfection.	Ins ⬜ Outs
Afterlife	19. There is a state of eternal punishment called hell.	Ins ⬜ Outs
God	13. There are three Persons in one God.	Ins ⬜ Outs
Christ	15. Christ is really present in the Eucharist.	Ins ⬜ Outs
Afterlife	9. There is a state of eternal reward called heaven.	Ins ⬜ Outs
Man	6. Every man has an immortal, spiritual soul.	Ins ⬜ Outs
Man	10. Man has a free will and is responsible for his actions, both good and evil.	Ins ⬜ Outs
God	3. There is a God.	Ins ⬜ Outs
Christ	5. Christ rose from the dead.	Ins ⬜ Outs
	Average of 20 items	Ins ⬜ Outs

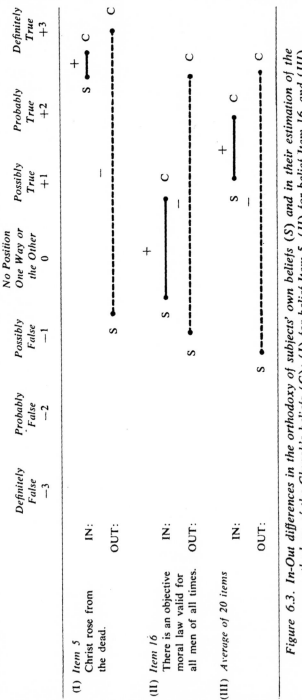

Figure 6.3. In-Out differences in the orthodoxy of subjects' own beliefs (S) and in their estimation of the orthodoxy of the Church's beliefs (C): (I) for belief Item 5, (II) for belief Item 16, and (III) for the average of the twenty belief items. For the full wording of each belief item, see Figure 6.3.

approximating the Church's position. On the other hand, there are beliefs, in particular "There is an objective moral law valid for all men of all times" (Figure 6.3 (II), Item 16) that the In will not compromise on. This belief is not as ambiguous as the former: one's concrete experience in life can lead in the direction of confirming or disproving it. Hence, to produce consistency between himself and his perception of the Church, the In makes the Church approximate his position. This approximation leads to the situation described in Chapter 4: those items that discriminate better between Ins and Outs in Table 6.4 (Perception of the Church's Beliefs) tend to be those that are the poorer discriminants in Table 4.1 (Self's Beliefs). Items 5 and 16 are the extreme cases, Item 5 being the best "Self" discriminant and the poorest "Church" discriminant, Item 16 being the poorest "Self" discriminant and the best "Church" discriminant.

Outs simply put the greatest distance between what they believe and what they feel the Church believes, doing this by moving themselves and the Church in opposite directions. In both extreme cases (Items 5 and 16), Out beliefs and perceptions of the Church's beliefs are in nearly the same dissociated positions.

These pushes and pulls, and, we must assume, enough variety in the Catholic Church (neither group saw it as monolithic), seem enough to produce these differing conceptions of what the Church believes, Ins thinking of the Church as less orthodox, Outs considering it more orthodox.

Perception of the Change in the Church

When Ins and Outs were asked to describe the change in the Church, there appeared to be little difference between the two groups. Below are some of their responses to the question, "What is the change that is going on in the Church? Sum up your understanding of it in a sentence or two":

a healthy rethinking and re-evaluation of what has previously been accepted as dogma   (In)

deciding whether to remain formally Catholic or to be Christian-Catholic   (In)

becoming more oriented toward laymen in it; widening its doors to admit people of other beliefs   (In)

trying to discover out of its own contemporary experience the significance of the Incarnation and Redemption—a process of getting rid of formulations that may at one time have been adequate but that are now frozen and irrelevant   (In)

the institution is becoming much more concerned with contemporary society than with the hereafter   (In)

people are starting to be honest in their theology as a description of life   (In)

an admission that Luther was right four hundred years ago; a beginning of rapprochement with the realities of the world   (Out)

a natural reaction to a closed institution—what happens to any closed institution   (Out)

a struggle between people willing to change and those who are willing to risk only in ways risked before (Out)

deciding whether to be relevant, worldly or other-worldly, fascist or liberal   (Out)

the Church is losing its political power slowly, coming to appreciate free conscience more and more (Out)

trying to evolve into an institution encompassing man's present-day way of life   (Out)

Six Outs (and one In) represented the change as superficial or insincere, depicting it, for example, as follows:[3]

> slow and unwilling change toward recognizing that people have their own needs and wants (Out)

> mainly liturgical window-dressing to satisfy the desires of educated Catholics (Out)

> facelifting job so it won't look so absurd to the world (Out)

Both Ins and Outs regard the change as highly positive (Table 6.7) and both see it originating within the Church rather than outside it (Table 6.5). When looking only within the Church, however, more Ins than Outs say the laity is responsible for the change, Outs tending to say the hierarchy and the clergy are the source. As far as doctrinal development is concerned, Outs maintain that it originates with the hierarchy and is imposed from above. Ins, on the other hand, see the hierarchy and the lower clergy as equally responsible for the development of doctrine, with the laity involved as well. No differences between the groups are evident when they are asked where the most resistance to the change is—nearly half of each group locates it solely within the hierarchy.

Agreement continues when, in answer to the question "What should the Catholic Church be?," Ins and Outs set forth their idea of the desired outcome of change:

> a community of people who use their belief in God and the redemptive act to really love all men as their brothers and to direct the world to an optimistic and positive solution of its problems (In)

3. See Appendix II, p. 248, Question 29. The two judges agreed 98 per cent of the time in coding a response "superficial or insincere change," responses disagreed upon being coded "not indicative of superficial or insincere change."

Table 6.5. In-Out Differences in the Perception of the Source of Doctrinal Development and Change in the Catholic Church

	Ins (N)	Outs (N)	χ^2, df, p
"In whose hands is the development of doctrine in the Church? Who, primarily, is responsible for it?"			
(1) The hierarchy	16	38	
(2) The hierarchy and the clergy	5	6	
(3) The clergy	16	4	
(4) The laity, or combination of the laity and the above	10	2	$\chi^2 = 24.58$ $df = 4$
(5) Other	3	0	$p < .001$
"What is the source of the impetus for change in the Church?"			
(1) Outside the Church	14	7	$\chi^2 = 4.54$
(2) Within the Church	28	38	$df = 2$
(3) Other or both	8	5	N.S.
Segment of membership most responsible for change			
(1) The hierarchy	3	7	
(2) The clergy	7	17	
(3) The laity	12	2	$\chi^2 = 16.42$
(4) Combinations of the above	17	20	$df = 4$
(5) Other, including no segment most responsible	11	4	$p < .005$
"Where is the most resistance to it (the change)?"			
(1) The hierarchy	21	23	
(2) The clergy	2	1	
(3) The laity	1	4	$\chi^2 = 3.89$
(4) Combinations of the above	11	13	$df = 4$
(5) Other, including no segment most responsible	15	9	N.S.

Note: See Appendix II, pp. 247–248, Questions 21–24. Coding procedure was identical with that described in Table 6.2, the judges agreeing 93.5 per cent of the time. *Hierarchy* included "pope," "cardinals," "bishops," "the Council," "Curia," "higher clergy," "the top." *Clergy* included "priests," "religious," "theologians," "scholars," "seminarians," "lower clergy." *Laity* included "the faithful," "lay theologians."

an all-encompassing, universal type thing big enough for anyone who wants to make the effort to be in (In)

characterized by people willing to serve; a visible community dedicated to serving other people; should be inspired by love of Christ to do this (In)

a group of people who take life seriously and wish to make use of the creative possibilities life offers (In)

a body that is representative of many different types of views but has a common sense of purpose in affecting a new world of peace (In)

much more freely structured and far less dogmatic than it is at present (Out)

a community of people who can interact reasonably and interact with society (Out)

a different answer for each country. It *should* be a revolutionary device (Out)

a group of people who happen to have the same beliefs rather than an organization that tells people what to believe (Out)

consistent with its principles; it should be in the vanguard of social change; it should develop community (Out)

Five Outs (and no Ins) have as an ideal a broken or nonexistent Church.

An idea of what Ins would like the Church to move away from can be gathered from their replies to an earlier question: "Is there anything else about the Church that you especially dislike or find not admirable?" A total of fourteen made clear mention of the hierarchy, ten of "authoritarianism," eight of "formalism," six of an "overinvolvement in bu-

Table 6.6. In-Out Differences Concerning Future Change in the Catholic Church

Statement No. and Type	Mean Ins	Mean Outs	Mean In-Out Diff.	F	p <
25 Conservative	.18	−1.88	2.06	31.97	.0001
22 Conservative	−1.66	−2.20	.54	3.74	.0560
21 Liberal	.94	1.44	−.50	2.49	.1179
23 Liberal	1.90	2.26	−.36	1.75	.1887
24 Conservative	−1.96	−2.22	.26	1.07	.3039
26 Liberal	2.54	2.50	.04	.04	.8368
Average Liberal Score	1.47	2.08	−.61	16.78	.0001

Note: Items are arranged in order of *F* values, which indicate the degree to which the distribution of In scores is different from the distribution of Out scores. In computing the Average Liberal Score, responses to Items 22, 24, and 25 were multiplied by −1. For the full wording of each item, see Figure 6.4.

reaucracy."[4] It seems that Ins wish the Church to be less the Church depicted by the Outs (the powerful clerical hierarchy) and more the Church they themselves describe (the community of people).

Figure 6.4 and Table 6.6 present subjects' quantified opinions on courses of action that the Church should adopt in the future. As can be seen, Ins are significantly differentiated from Outs on only one item, Ins being indifferent to the Church's "mission to bring all people into her fold" and Outs rejecting it. Outs are, on the whole, more liberal (as liberal is defined by these items). This effect is contributed to largely by the difference in the "mission" item just referred to. It also appears to mean, though, that one is liberal about an organiza-

4. See Appendix II, p. 215, Question 27. The two judges agreed on 80 per cent of the cases, the ones disagreed upon being categorized "other."

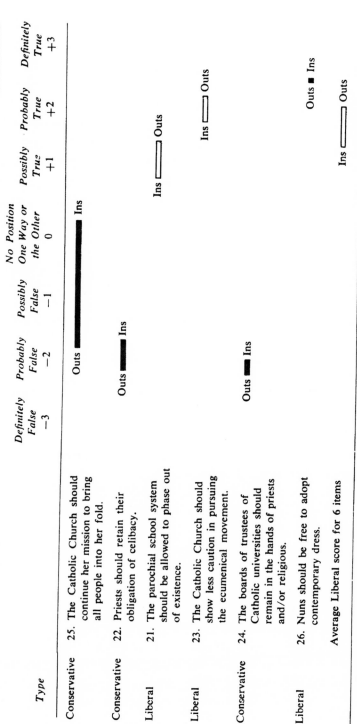

Figure 6.4. In-Out differences concerning future change in the Catholic Church. The bar represents the size of the mean In-Out difference. Items are arranged in order of F values (see Table 6.6).

tion he has left behind because he has no real stake in it or because, in some instances, liberalism means a disintegration of the organization (for example, "The parochial school system should be allowed to phase out of existence.") On five of six specific issues, however, Ins and Outs are not far apart in their opinion of what the Church should become.

If Ins and Outs are fairly uniform in their description of the change and their expression of its desired outcome, they disagree when appraising its chances of success, Ins being much more optimistic than Outs. Ins believe more strongly, too, that people like themselves have the power to be agents of future change in the Church (Table 6.7).

Finally, an assessment of the effect of change in the Church on a person's In-Out status yields the conclusion that the majority of Ins find the change supportive and none find it problematic (Table 6.7). Of the thirty-four I asked informally if they would be out were it not for the change, nine said "Yes" or "Possibly-Probably Yes," three could not answer, and twenty-two said "No" or "Possibly-Probably No." The change, apparently, creates room for some of the Ins to remain members.

Most of the Outs find innovations in the Church having little effect on their status as ex-members, and two say it actually confirms their position (Table 6.7). More than one might think, however, say the change is forcing them to re-evaluate themselves. Presumably, the very things that alienated them are slowly disappearing, and they find fewer reasons for remaining out.

As far as the change in the Church goes, then, more Outs than Ins feel it is being imposed from above. Other than that, the two groups see it the same way and consider it for the good. Both groups have roughly the same ideals for the Church, but the Ins are more optimistic about the possibility of attaining them and about their role in the mechanisms of change. Several Ins feel they would be out were it not for the

Table 6.7. In-Out Differences in the Evaluation of Change in the Catholic Church

"What should the Catholic Church be? . . .	Ins (N)	Outs (N)	χ^2, df, p
. . . Can it ever become that?"			
(1) Yes	23	9	
(2) Neither yes nor no, or yes or no qualified	22	27	$\chi^2 = 12.78$
(3) No	0	5	$df = 3$
(4) Question does not apply (because Church is the ideal or the ideal is negative)	5	9	$p < .01$
INS: "Do you have power in helping bring that about?" OUTS: "Would you have had any such power had you remained a member?"			
(1) Yes	30	7	
(2) Neither yes nor no, or yes or no qualified	13	16	$\chi^2 = 26.52$ $df = 3$
(3) No	4	18	$p < .001$
(4) Question does not apply	3	9	
"Overall, do you consider the change to be positive or negative?"			
(1) Positive	49	43	$\chi^2 = 5.06$
(2) Neither or both	1	5	$df = 2$
(3) Negative	0	2	N.S.
"How does the change affect your status of being *in* or *out?*"			
(1) Confirms status	37	2	$\chi^2 = 54.37$
(2) Forces questioning of status	0	10	$df = 2$
(3) Other or no effect	13	38	$p < .001$
"Does it make you feel comfortable or uneasy about being *in* or *out?*"			
(1) Comfortable	40	7	$\chi^2 = 44.70$
(2) Neither or both	8	40	$df = 2$
(3) Uneasy	2	3	$p < .001$

Note: See Appendix II, pp. 248–249, Questions 25, 27, 28, 30, 31, 35. Coding procedure for the first, second, and fourth questions was similar to that described in Table 6.2, the judges agreeing 92 per cent, 95.5 per cent, and 88 per cent of the time, respectively.

change, and several Outs find the change a reason for questioning their status.

Perception of the Criteria of Membership in the Church

A further demarcation between In and Out perceptions of the Church was expected to be their appraisal of its borderline, i.e., their assessment of precisely what it was that signed an In as in and an Out as out. Outs were expected to have a rigidly defined borderline and that of Ins was anticipated to be rather loose.

Table 6.8 provides little support for this expectation. Baptism is a major criterion for Ins defining themselves as mem-

Table 6.8. In-Out Differences in the Perception of the Criteria of Membership in the Catholic Church

	Ins (N)	Outs (N)	χ^2, df, p
"By what criteria do you consider yourself *in* or *out* of the Church? Is one of the criteria a matter of . . .			
. . . being baptized?"			
(1) Yes	34		
(2) Neither yes nor no, or yes or no qualified	8	Does not	
(3) No	8	apply	
". . . religious practice?"			
(1) Yes	28	37	
(2) Neither yes nor no, or yes or no			$\chi^2 = 4.25$
qualified	10	4	$df = 2$
(3) No	12	9	N.S.
". . . believing what the Church teaches?"			
(1) Yes	26	41	
(2) Neither yes nor no, or yes or no			$\chi^2 = 11.48$
qualified	14	3	$df = 2$
(3) No	10	6	$p < .005$
". . . moral practice?"			
(1) Yes	9	30	
(2) Neither yes nor no, or yes or no			$\chi^2 = 18.80$
qualified	13	5	$df = 2$
(3) No	28	15	$p < .001$

Table 6.8.—Continued

	Ins (N)	Outs (N)	χ^2, df, p
"If a Catholic got a divorce and remarried, would you still consider him a member of the Catholic Church?"			
(1) Yes	21	13	
(2) Neither yes nor no, or yes or no qualified	12	5	$\chi^2 = 9.43$
(3) No	6	10	$df = 3$
(4) Yes, if he so considered himself	11	22	$p < .025$
"If a Catholic openly professed a belief in opposition to the official teaching of the Church, would you still consider him a member of the Church?"			
(1) Yes	28	19	
(2) Neither yes nor no, or yes or no qualified	6	1	
(3) No	2	7	$\chi^2 = 18.16$
(4) Yes, if he so considered himself	5	19	$df = 4$
(5) Depends on the belief involved	9	4	$p < .005$
"If a Catholic did not attend Mass for five years, would you still consider him a member of the Church?"			
(1) Yes	15	5	
(2) Neither yes nor no, or yes or no qualified	17	5	$\chi^2 = 25.82$
(3) No	13	14	$df = 3$
(4) Yes, if he so considered himself	5	26	$p < .001$
"If a Catholic were excommunicated from the Church, would you still consider him a member of the Church?"			
(1) Yes	15	9	
(2) Neither yes nor no, or yes or no qualified	7	4	
(3) No	11	23	
(4) Yes, if he so considered himself	8	14	$\chi^2 = 17.20$
(5) Depends on the reasons for excommunication	9	0	$df = 4$ $p < .005$

Note: See Appendix II, p. 249, Questions 36–40, and p. 250, Questions 46–49.

bers; only about half of them think of religious practice or orthodoxy in belief as a gauge, and less than a fifth say they consider themselves members because of moral practice. Belief, religious practice, and moral practice, on the other hand, are all touchstones against which the majority of Outs define themselves as ex-members. That more Outs than Ins consider these criteria definitive with respect to themselves might lead one to conclude that they perceive the borderline more rigidly.

But Out replies to the next four questions belie this interpretation. In hypothetical instances of a Catholic getting a divorce, professing a belief in opposition to the official teaching of the Church, not attending Mass for five years, and being excommunicated, Outs are generally willing to consider the party still a member of the Catholic Church if he so regards himself. The main In-Out difference in this series of questions is that Ins say "Yes" to considering the party a member and Outs say "Yes, if he wishes to be." Both Ins and Outs see divorce or openly professing an opposing belief as less reason for considering a Catholic out of the Church than failing to attend Mass for five years or excommunication. It is interesting that only eleven Ins and twenty-three Outs unequivocally regard as out of the Church someone under the ban of excommunication.

Perhaps the most intriguing question in the entire interview was, "Could someone else believe what you believe, or do what you do, and still consider himself (In) (Out of) the Church?" Ins were asked if someone else could consider himself out, and Outs if someone else could consider himself in. Only twenty Ins and twenty-three Outs responded "No" to this question, meaning that more than half of each group felt it was possible to consider itself on the other side of the fence. While Outs used the criteria of religious practice, belief, and moral practice to consider themselves out, they seemed to realize they need not do so. Thus, both Ins and Outs perceived the borderline as the vague place it was assumed to be at the start of this investigation.

It seems appropriate at this point to present the data on subjects' actual religious practice. It was reported in Chapter 3 that, for forty Outs, a "concrete act by which you gave up membership" was ceasing to attend Mass and/or the sacraments. Thirty-seven Outs (Table 6.8) later said they felt a failure to practice their religion was an indicator that they were out. Slightly more than half the Ins agree that religious practice is an important criterion. Are the two groups as different in their religious practice as these statements might indicate?

Table 6.9 reveals that they are. Attendance at Mass, the reception of Communion, and Confession are all excellent discriminants between Ins and Outs: indeed, religious practice is one of the best discriminants that can be found. Forty-two Ins attend Mass at least weekly while only one Out does. No Out has been to Confession in the past year, while thirty-eight Ins have gone at least once. Religious practice is more

Table 6.9. In-Out Differences in Actual Religious Practice

Mass	Ins (N)	Outs (N)	χ^2, df, p
(1) Never	0	12	
(2) Less than weekly	8	37	$\chi^2 = 69.81$
(3) Weekly	32	1	$df = 3$
(4) More than weekly	10	0	$p < .001$
Communion			
(1) Never	0	38	
(2) Less than weekly	13	11	$\chi^2 = 72.31$
(3) Weekly	27	1	$df = 3$
(4) More than weekly	10	0	$p < .001$
Confession			
(1) Never	12	50	
(2) Less than monthly	32	0	$\chi^2 = 61.29$
(3) Monthly	3	0	$df = 3$
(4) More than monthly	3	0	$p < .001$

Note: "Never" means never in the past year or since leaving the Church.

a criterion than Ins realize, though it is still possible to find an In practicing only minimally.

Summary

Two Churches, with some degree of overlap, are delineated by subjects in this study. One, the institutional Church perceived by the Outs, is centered around a powerful clerical hierarchy who impose change from above. It is rigid, conservative, dogmatic, and orthodox. What change it has shown has made several Outs question their status. The other, the people's Church perceived by the Ins, is centered around God and the members, but still encompasses a less powerful clerical hierarchy. It is more flexible and liberal, less dogmatic and orthodox than the Church of the Outs. It also has a brighter future: its members have the power to move the Church away from the hierarchy and toward the people. This possibility, and the change that has taken place already, creates room for some of the Ins to remain members.

Membership in each of these Churches is, to a large extent, determined by a person's own criteria, although religious practice turns out to be more an empirical criterion for membership than some Ins realize.

These different and rather consistent portraits of the Catholic Church are drawn by people with the same prolonged exposure to it. Perhaps because of the variety of schools in it, the Church demands that it be selectively perceived. Why Ins select one element and Outs another is a question we shall approach in the section that follows.

PART III

The Search for Why

SEVEN

Male versus Female

As a pause before entering the realm of explanation and as a prelude to it, it would be well to re-analyze the data presented up to this point to see what characteristics vary with the sex of the respondent. Demographic information should be the first to be examined to see if there is an equal or near-equal representation of the sexes on each variable. Failure to do so might lead us to attribute to sex what in reality is an effect of an unobserved co-variant of sex. Once this matter is attended to, male and female accounts of the period of change, their statements of what they believe and what they value, and their representations of the Catholic Church can be inspected for the occurrence of sex differences. Those that appear can subsequently be compared with findings from psychological research on sex differences.

Demography: The Graduate School Difference

In the data appearing in Chapter 2, there are few statistically significant ($p < .05$) effects associated with the sex of subjects.[1] There are no significant differences in the two sexes' perception of me (the interviewer [Table 2.2]), in their citizenship, age, marital status, number of children, ethnicity, family background (Table 2.3), or in their starting point with respect to Catholicism, both as they reflect upon it (Figure 2.1, Times A and B) and, with one slight exception, as it is measured by more overt indices (Table 2.6). The exception is that fewer male Outs (sixteen) than female Outs (twenty-three) report full time attendance at a Catholic grammar school (the figures for male and female Ins are twenty and twenty-two, respectively). This Out difference should not be of serious concern, however, as only three males, compared with one female, report no attendance at a Catholic elementary school.

Males and females, of course, often attended different Catholic colleges or universities (Table 2.4), and the question of whether coeducational institutions had effects different from all-male or all-female colleges is an important one. Among males there are no consistent associations between the kind of undergraduate college attended and subjects' current status, beliefs, or perceptions of the Church. Female Ins (sixteen of twenty-five) tended to come from all-female colleges, and to a lesser extent, female Outs from coeducational colleges (fourteen of twenty-five), but this association is far from statistical significance. There are no consistent relationships, either, between the type of undergraduate institutions and a female subject's present beliefs or perceptions of the Church. All-male and all-female colleges do not appear, then, to be significant socializing agents for sex differences in religious orientation.

More female Outs (fourteen) had an annual income above $5000 than did male Outs (four) (Table 2.3), whose income

1. Throughout this chapter, any differences between groups or subgroups that are spoken of are significant at the .05 level unless otherwise indicated in the text. The reader is referred to Appendix I for the meaning associated with the phrase, "a significant difference."

level was almost identical with that of male and female Ins. Twenty-one female Outs mentioned a north central state as their place of birth (Table 2.3), a number significantly higher than male Outs (ten), who again paralleled male and female Ins in their reported place of birth. These two differences reflect the fact that a number of female Outs were not drawn from the graduate school at Northwestern or Chicago (Table 2.5).

As explained in Chapter 2, female Outs were drawn from outside the graduate schools because enough of them were not found within the schools. While it is possible that female Outs were less public about their status than other subjects, a more reasonable conclusion—because it ties in with evidence presented below—is that there were simply fewer of them to be located, that females, in other words, are less likely than males to leave the Catholic Church.

The presence among the female Outs of thirteen who never attended graduate school complicates the interpretation of differences associated with sex. If female Outs are different from the other three groups, is this caused by the fact that they are female and out, or might it be because a number of them never attended graduate school? Graduate schools, presumably, select certain kinds of individuals and/or change them after their arrival.

To see if graduate school did make a difference among female Outs, a comparison was made of those twelve who were in graduate school or at least had taken some graduate courses with the thirteen who had never taken a graduate course. The comparisons were made on eighty-three variables identified through previous handling of the data as the more important ones.

Of the eighty-three comparisons made, only four revealed differences significant at the .05 level: nongraduate-school female Outs were more liberal regarding what the Church should do in the future (Figure 6.4), and they were more rejecting of three beliefs (Figure 4.1), one about Christ's resurrection, the second about Mary's assumption, and the third about original sin. Averaging across all twenty beliefs, the nongraduate-school female Outs were more disapproving, though the mean difference was slight and not statistically significant.

Basically, then, these two subgroups are not far apart, perhaps because the female Outs with no graduate school were drawn from the fringes of the graduate school community or had intentions themselves of entering graduate school. The most important of the discrepancies that do come up, the three involving beliefs, do not cause us to draw any false conclusions about sex differences: those female Outs not in graduate school were more like the male Outs than were the females in graduate school. Hence, the gap between the sexes is diminished, not enlarged, by including among the female Outs thirteen who had never been to graduate school.

For male subjects, an analysis of variance was computed for eighty-three key variables to determine what effects were associated with their being at Northwestern University or the University of Chicago. Two significant status × school interaction effects were found in the area of belief (Figure 4.1), two in subjects' Value-Instrumentality scores (Table 5.3), one in the statements concerning the course of action the Church should adopt in the future (Figure 6.4), and two among those variables relating to perception of one's parents (Chapter 8). The only effect with any important meaning is that male Ins from Northwestern are a bit more orthodox (though not significantly so) than the ones from Chicago. Overall, however, there are few differences associated with the graduate school of the male respondent.

In summary, there is only a slight unevenness in the sexes' representation on demographic variables. What inequality there is appears related, in part, to the fact that some female Outs were not graduate students. However, graduate school status does not appear to be an important factor with either of the sexes: among males, which graduate school they attended is of little significance, and, among females, whether they had been to graduate school has little effect. We can proceed in our analysis, then, knowing that male-female differences are not attributable to any unnoticed co-variant of sex.

The Period of Change

Female Outs appear to have entered upon a critical period of change later in life than male Outs. Fourteen of the females, as compared with twenty-one of the males, reported that their re-evaluation began before or during college, whereas eleven females and only four males said it did not begin until after college. Only seven females (versus sixteen males) said the crisis was resolved by the end of their college years. Consequently, when looking back upon their senior year of college, female Outs rate the positive importance of Catholicism significantly higher than do male Outs (Figure 2.1, Time C).

Male and female Ins do not differ as in the above case. The majority of each group began to re-examine its position in college and presently does not regard the process as terminated. Their evaluations of the positive importance of Catholicism in college are the same.

Five male Outs said they had turned to atheism, while no female Outs did. Conversely, eleven females and only five males stated they had now adopted "a personal religion." More females (twelve) than males (five) felt they had lost some security or stability in leaving the Church, males (sixteen, versus seven females) usually saying they had lost nothing.

In the course of enlisting interviewees, I encountered seven females who were so ambivalent about their current status that they could not define themselves as either in or out of the Church (and, consequently, could not be interviewed). Only one male was so ambivalent. At the beginning of each scheduled interview, subjects were asked if they wished to qualify their In or Out status in any way: among Outs, nineteen females, as opposed to ten males, made some qualification.

Female Outs also think of Catholicism more positively at the present time than do male Outs (Figure 2.1, Time D), and fewer of them are closed to the idea of ever returning to Catholicism, though this latter sex difference is not statistically significant.

Among Ins, fewer females (four) than males (nine) considered leaving a real possibility as they underwent change, and four females (no males) said their reasons for being a member had not changed at all. Currently, female Ins are less open about the possibility of ever leaving the Church, though this male-female difference does not attain statistical significance.

It is interesting to note that, in thirteen of the female case histories (five Ins, eight Outs), a serious personal relationship with a male (dating, an affair, engagement, marriage) either created the crisis of examination or helped prolong it. Only two males (one In, one Out) reported the reverse. In a number of instances, a husband or future husband had already left the Church and influenced his wife in the same direction. On several occasions, a male or female was engaged or almost engaged to someone of different religious persuasions, and in one case a female was deeply affected by a man who was an atheist. When there was an indication of influence between the sexes, it was always from male to female, there being no examples of the reverse.

A rather consistent picture is being drawn: females are less likely than males to leave the Church; they are slower to do so; females who have left are more religious than males who have left, and they are not as certain about the permanency of their position outside the Church. They are more likely to be influenced by males in the process of change than males are by them.

What They Believe

Table 7.1 shows that five belief formulas discriminate significantly between the sexes, females being more orthodox in their replies than males. For the average of all twenty beliefs, the effect for sex is significant at the .0196 level. Female Ins are more orthodox than male Ins on eighteen of the twenty beliefs; the groups are equal on one, and the females are even more rejecting (−2.00) than males (−1.56) on the item having to do with contraception (Item 20). Female Outs are less negative than male Outs on sixteen items; they are tied with males on one and more negative on three, the major difference appearing on the belief having to do with free will (Item 10; males +1.96; females +1.44).

Of the five statements that discriminate between the sexes at the .05 level or better, four are of the "God and the Other World" type, ambiguous beliefs against which psychological differences should come to the fore. Seven of the nine poorest sex discriminants (not shown in Table 7.1) are of the "Man and This World" type.

What They Value

Fewer differences than expected are evident in the two sexes' expression of what matters to them in life. On the

Table 7.1. Significant Sex Differences in the Acceptance of Twenty Beliefs

| Belief No. and Type | In | | Out | | F for Sex Effect | p < |
	Male	Female	Male	Female		
3 God	2.68	2.88	.16	1.80	20.03	.0001
6 Man	1.92	2.72	− .44	.64	11.35	.0011
17 Mary	.20	1.40	−1.72	−1.04	9.55	.0027
15 Christ	2.08	2.56	−1.36	− .56	5.85	.0175
5 Christ	2.44	2.72	−1.36	− .56	5.51	.0211
Average of 20 items	.70	1.11	−1.41	−1.02	5.64	.0196

Note: Items are arranged in order of *F* values, which indicate the degree to which the distribution of male scores is different from the distribution of female scores. For Item 3 the Status × Sex effect is significant with *p* < .0008. For the full wording of each item, see Figure 4.1.

open-ended value questions, there is a nonsignificant tendency for females to show more concern for fulfillment in the personal and interpersonal areas and to express admiration for a parent instead of a public, historical, or literary figure. In subscribing to the twenty listed values (Figure 5.2), males are significantly more interested in "making a significant contribution in the intellectual community," and male Ins and female Outs are more interested than the other two groups in "accomplishing something for the cause of world peace." Other than that there are no significant discrepancies in the sexes' description of what they value.

There is only one sex difference in subjects' ratings of the instrumentality of membership in attaining the values (Figure 5.3): females see membership as more of a hindrance to "escaping the confines of my early background." Two significant effects appear in the Value-Instrumentality scores, but the scores of each group are so low that the differences are of little importance. No significant sex effects are seen in the ΣVI score, indicating overall positive or negative feeling toward the Church, or in the $\Sigma|VI| - |\Sigma VI|$ score, intended to be a measure of ambivalence toward membership in the Church.

In all, there are few differences in the sexes' statement of what they value or of how the Church relates to the values. On sixty-seven of the seventy-two variables involved, there are no significant main or interacting effects associated with sex.

Their Perception of the Church

The largest discrepancy between the sexes is manifest in their estimation of the "thinking of the Church" on twenty items of belief. Table 7.2 lists fourteen beliefs on which male and female responses are significantly different and indicates that the sex difference averaged over all twenty beliefs is significant at the .0006 level. On every item the male In sees the

Table 7.2. Significant Sex Differences in the Perception of the "Thinking of the Church" on Twenty Beliefs

Belief No. and Type	In Male	In Female	Out Male	Out Female	F for Sex Effect	p <
13 God	2.20	3.00	2.76	3.00	11.89	.0009
16 Morality	.20	1.60	2.12	2.68	11.52	.0011
8 Morality	.44	1.40	1.44	2.60	10.28	.0019
20 Morality	.28	1.20	1.00	2.24	10.23	.0019
17 Mary	1.40	2.20	2.32	2.92	8.44	.0046
19 Afterlife	1.84	2.40	2.28	2.96	8.00	.0058
15 Christ	2.48	2.96	2.84	2.96	7.85	.0062
14 Man	.52	1.48	2.00	2.48	6.59	.0118
5 Christ	2.80	3.00	2.84	3.00	5.82	.0178
7 Mary	1.64	2.40	2.56	2.76	5.73	.0187
18 Man	2.12	2.56	2.60	2.96	5.67	.0193
6 Man	2.52	2.96	2.84	3.00	5.33	.0232
12 Morality	1.64	2.24	2.40	2.80	5.07	.0267
4 Morality	1.20	1.60	1.92	2.68	4.09	.0459
Average of 20 items	1.64	2.24	2.33	2.79	12.90	.0006

Note: Items are arranged in order of *F* values, which indicate the degree to which the distribution of male scores is different from the distribution of female scores. For the full wording of each item, see Figure 6.2.

Church as less orthodox than the female In, and the male Out sees the Church as less orthodox than the female Out. Figure 7.1 shows the typical position taken by the In and Out of each sex in describing his own (S) and the Church's (C) beliefs.

Among Outs, females define the Church as more visible and perceive it as more monolithic, conservative, dogmatic, and otherworldly than males. Although originally less likely to leave the Church and presently more subtly tied to it, female Outs overtly describe the Church as less desirable. The inner attitude and overt description evidence a greater need for cognitive consistency and a type of global perception: the Church is seen as one completely negative entity. Male Outs, in contrast, while considering the Church undesirable, are not

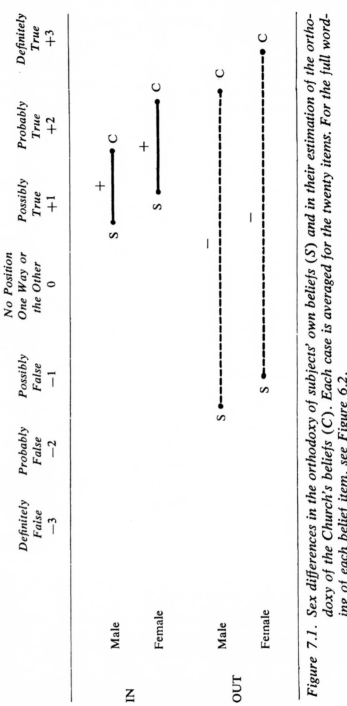

Figure 7.1. Sex differences in the orthodoxy of subjects' own beliefs (S) and in their estimation of the ortho-doxy of the Church's beliefs (C). Each case is averaged for the twenty items. For the full word-ing of each belief item, see Figure 6.2.

as totally negative in their descriptions of it. They are still able to acknowledge some positive elements in the Church.

Male and female Ins do not differ in their responses to these quantified descriptions of the Church, though females lean slightly toward perceiving the Church as more monolithic, conservative, etc. Perhaps being more orthodox themselves, they can perceive the Church as a more orthodox, conservative collectivity. A small exception in the case of both Ins and Outs is that a female of either group thinks the Church more liberal regarding the dress of nuns.

That female Outs are more subtly tied to the Church than male Outs is demonstrated, too, in that more of them want something to remain unchanged in the Church and that more of them say the change in the Church does affect their status, usually to make them question it (see Table 6.7).

Females' perception of the borderline around the Church seems more fixed than that of males. In saying whether Baptism, religious practice, belief, or moral practice is a defining criterion, more females than males in each group answer "Yes." The differences are statistically significant in two of the seven cases (Ins, regarding Baptism; Outs, regarding religious practice; see Table 6.8).

As far as actual religious practice goes (Table 6.9), male and female Ins are not distinguished, but male and female Outs are. Only one female Out has not attended Mass at all in the past year (or since leaving) and only fifteen have not received Communion. The figures for males are eleven and twenty-three, respectively.

Summarizing the major sex differences, we find that In and Out females are more religious than their male counterparts, at least as that term is conventionally understood and measured. Females are slower to leave the Church and more bound to it even if they do leave. They perceive the Church in a more orthodox way, with female Outs seeing it more globally negative than male Outs.

Related Evidence and Hints of Explanation

A number of studies have confirmed that women are more religious than men. This was found to be the case in a group of post-World War II college students (Allport et al., 1948), and it usually happens when men and women take the Allport-Vernon-Lindzey Study of Values (Allport et al., 1960). Figures on religious practice among Catholics in France, Germany, Belgium, Holland, and parts of Italy (around 1952) show a greater percentage of women than men attending Mass (Fogarty, 1957). Three national surveys in the United States (1957 and 1958) found forty-six percent of Protestant women reporting regular Church attendance while only thirty percent of the Protestant men did, and seventy-five percent of Catholic women reporting regular attendance, compared with sixty-seven percent of the Catholic men (Lazerwitz, 1964).[2]

A more recent (1963–64) national survey of American Catholics between twenty-three and fifty-seven years of age yielded findings in the same vein (Greeley and Rossi, 1966). With parental religiousness, level of education, and amount of Catholic schooling held constant, the sex of the respondent was a good predictor of sacramental activity and membership in voluntary Catholic organizations, with females being higher on these indices. To a lesser degree, sex distinguished responses on the Church-as-teacher, religious knowledge, doctrinal orthodoxy, ethical orthodoxy, and sexual mores indices, with women always being higher on these measures. An interesting sidelight was that religious differences between the sexes decreased if only those respondents who had attended Catholic colleges were compared. Apparently, the effect of Catholic colleges on the men interviewed was to bring them close to the level of religious activity and belief shown by their femi-

---

2. Jewish men, however, attend synagogue 2½ times as often as Jewish women, a result, says Lazerwitz, of the Orthodox Jewish norm emphasizing male attendance.

nine confreres. Thus, sex differences found in the present investigation can be assumed to be even wider in the Catholic population at large—that is, if what was true of Catholic colleges ten to twenty years ago still holds today.

Three possibilities can be suggested as explanations for the male-female difference in religious orientation. First, the association between religion and the female sex may be a cultural given into which youth are directly socialized in the same way that they are socialized into other sex-associated characteristics. At the other extreme is the position that religion as presented to the young is sexually neutral and that male-female differences in religiosity are mediated by other innate or acquired psychosexual characteristics. The point of view lying between these two extremes is that the female-religion association and other psychological characteristics of the female are interdependent and mutually reinforcing. It would assume that, however the interplay between the psychological and the sociological originated, religion has been culturally feminized by the psychological characteristics of women and consequently attracts more women than men to it. The presence of more women, of course, increases the feminization and makes the female-religion association more of a cultural given. Religion may also serve to increase in women those psychological characteristics typically associated with their sex.

If psychological differences between the sexes, then, are responsible in whole or part for differences in religious orientation, it would be well to look in detail at some of the outstanding psychological differences and ascertain whether they might not account for some of the phenomena reported in this chapter. What are some of the major documented sex characteristics?[3]

3. An excellent summary of research on sex differences, and one that proved invaluable to me, is the 1966 volume edited by Eleanor E. Maccoby, *The Development of Sex Differences.*

For one thing, there is consistent evidence that females are more dependent than males. No uniform sex differences have been observed at the early years, but in high school and college, girls regularly score higher on self-report and projective measures of dependency (Maccoby, 1966). In one longitudinal study, dependency was found to be more stable over time in growing females than in growing males (Kagan and Moss, 1962). A review of ethnographers' accounts of one hundred and ten cultures, the majority nonliterate, showed that eighty-seven per cent of them exert socialization pressure upon boys to achieve and eighty-five per cent to be self-reliant, while only three and zero per cent, respectively, exert the same pressure predominantly upon girls. Girls in these cultures are more often trained to be nurturant, responsible, and obedient (Barry et al., 1957). The greater independence and autonomy of male relative to female, then, appears to be a near-universal condition.

Males, in the present study, strike more independent action than females. They leave the Church with greater ease, beginning the process earlier and making a cleaner break in the end. Males who remain in the Church have thought more about actually leaving and are still more open to the possibility; they break more with tradition in their beliefs and are more inclined to define the Church and its beliefs as they wish and not as the "official" Church wishes. Male Outs, too, are less dependent on the "official" Church in estimating the Church's beliefs.

To the extent that belief in God involves a dependency, female Ins and Outs show more of this trait than their male counterparts. No female Out turned to atheism, whereas five males did, and females of either status agree to the formula "There is a God" with more certainty. Male independence can also explain why male Outs run contrary to form on the belief scale and show more agreement than females to "Man has a free will and is responsible for his actions both good and evil."

Related to the data on dependency is that on conformity and suggestibility. Several experimenters have compared men and women on their ability to withstand group pressure and report a perception contrary to the bogus consensus of the group. When sex differences appeared, women were more conforming to the group than were men, an effect observed even when members of the group were of the same sex as the subject. Findings of sex differences in studies of persuasive communication with high school and adult subjects have regularly pronounced females more susceptible to persuasive messages. Other studies, some using paper and pencil testing and others naturalistic observation, have found that females express more socially acceptable attitudes and, both on paper and in their actual behavior, are less inclined to break school or cultural rules (for summaries of all these studies, see Maccoby, 1966). The fifty females under consideration here are more likely to conform with the beliefs and regulations of their religious upbringing, and when influence is transmitted between the sexes, it is they who are on the receiving (or suggestible) end.

Women also have a greater need for affiliation, as manifested both in investigations of their fantasy material and in experiments that observe their overt behavior in groups. Younger girls have continually shown more concern for popularity than boys; girls and women are nearly always more nurturant; and in all but one of twenty-two studies summarized in a single volume (Maccoby, 1966), females were found to express greater interest in or more positive feelings for other persons.

Affiliative concern for her Catholic family might explain female reluctance to leave the Church or become less orthodox. Females in the present study do place more importance on interpersonal success in the open-ended value section of the questionnaire, and they are more likely than males to admire a parent instead of someone outside the family. If affiliation with one's family is a factor affecting religiosity, we would expect families less devotedly Catholic to produce more Outs, and we might hypothesize that this association is stronger for females. Data in Chapter 8 will provide a test of these expectations.

When tests such as the Childrens' Manifest Anxiety Scale, the General Anxiety Scale for Children, the Test Anxiety Scale for Children, and the Taylor Manifest Anxiety Scale have been given to both sexes any time from the age of six to adulthood, about half of the time no differences between male and female have been found, and the other half of the time females have scored higher (Maccoby, 1966). Two experiments using physiological measures also lend support to the findings of a greater tendency toward anxiety in females. One of these used measures of skin resistance, blood flow, blood pressure, and heart rate to discover that twelve-year-old girls reacted more to a brief stressful situation than did boys of the same age (Sontag, 1947). In a Galvanic-Skin-Response conditioning experiment, researchers found that women college students showed greater GSR reactivity than men in all their experimental conditions (Berry and Martin, 1957). In a religious context, when a group of ninth grade students in New England were asked, "Have you ever had a particular experience when you felt especially close to God?", more girls than boys reported experiences of being alone and experiences of anxiety and fear (Elkind and Elkind, 1962).

Retaining a belief system with a fear- or anxiety-inducing component is in some respects similar to an animal's retention of a response learned in a classical avoidance experiment. The animal retains its response even though the negatively reinforcing punishment never comes (Solomon et al., 1953). Many religious beliefs and practices have been conditioned to a fear of punishment in an afterlife. Such beliefs and practices appear to be very rigid because the believer has no way of knowing if punishment will indeed follow a violation of what he has been taught. Neither he nor the animal in the avoidance experiment wishes to take the chance that punishment will not follow a change in belief or behavior.

If such anxiety and fear produces rigidity in the belief system, and if females tend to exhibit more anxiety than males, perhaps this trait is another mediator of sex differences in religious orientation. Females, according to this explanation, show less religious change because they are more affected by the anxiety-inducing elements of the belief system. Female Outs in our study do say they miss the security and stability of being in the Church more than do male Outs, and females also tend to exhibit more questioning of their present status.

Also a part of the literature on sex differences are the slight, but rather constant, discrepancies uncovered in male and female cognitive styles. For one thing, boys and adult men in experimental problem-solving situations seem better able to overcome established mental sets, restructure problems, and discover short-term solutions (cf. Maccoby, 1966). Making arbitrary judgments of category width, girls and adult women are more conservative and tend to be more uncertain and less inclined to take a risk when making probability choices (Maccoby, 1966). On many occasions, males, especially those of college age and older, have proved to be more "field-independent" than women (Witkin et al., 1962). For example, in a totally darkened room, they are less distracted by a misleading rotating frame as they try to adjust a luminescent rod within the frame to true vertical. Or, presumably better able to ignore distracting lines, they are quicker to pick out figures embedded in patterns designed to mask the figure.

This greater susceptibility to contextual effects on the part of females has also been called "global responding" or a failure in "analytical thinking." The phenomenon appears to be reliable over time and consistent over a number of related tasks. There are also studies relating this characteristic of intellectual functioning to the qualities of conformity, suggestibility, and dependency mentioned earlier (see Maccoby, 1966). Apparently, field-dependent people find it harder to ignore stimuli that come from other people, stimuli that, like the rotating frame and the distracting lines, interrupt internal thought processes.

Global responding or field dependence seems to be evident in the case of the female Outs, who see the Church as more negative and orthodox than male Outs. Why female Ins do not see the Church in a more positive light than male Ins (as an extension of our reasoning would lead us to expect) is difficult to explain, but may be related to the fact that female Ins have not undergone the movement that female Outs have, and that females in general are less inclined than males to make independent definitions of the Church.

Other comparisons between our data and the results of these experiments on cognitive styles can be made only analogously. The experimental tasks are short-term, often games of one kind or another, and involve the perception of things. Subjects in the present investigation spoke of longer-term experiences that were hardly games and related perceptions of a social institution. Yet the similarities are there: males break with the heretofore more easily, take more risks when confronted with ambiguity, and depend more on internal cues than on stimuli in the field when making judgments.

It is a moot point whether the source of all these psychological differences is the biological makeup of the sexes or the different patterns of socialization they undergo. On the one hand, aggressiveness and other sex-associated behaviors have been related to the presence of sex hormones in rats and monkeys; sex-appropriate behaviors have been observed in field and laboratory studies of unsocialized infant monkeys; slight sex differences have been observed even in unsocialized human infants; and the vast majority of cultures assign behavior roles compatible with the greater physical size and strength of males and the child-bearing and nursing role of the female (Hamburg and Lunde, 1966; D'Andrade, 1966).

On the other hand, studies of hermaphrodites have led some to the conclusion that the human infant is psychosexually neutral at birth and that one's sex characteristics are almost entirely a matter of socialization practices (Hampson and Hampson, 1961). Persons whose sex assignment at birth was incorrect because of the ambiguous appearance of their external genitalia end up conforming to their assigned sex role, though chromosomally and hormonally they may be of the opposite sex. Even those whose predominant genital appearance contradicts their sex of assignment establish a gender role consistent with their rearing and do so without the occurrence of psychotic illness. This has led one theorist (Kohlberg, 1966) to suggest that gender identity, i.e., cognitive self-categorization as boy or girl, is the critical organizer of sex-role attitudes, and it is also consistent with the social-learning point of view that sex-typed behavior is acquired according to the same principles of reinforcement that any behavior is (Mischel, 1966).

Presumably, the sex differences in religious orientation uncovered here and the general psychological differences just reviewed are more a matter of environmental events than genetic makeup, but debate on this point need not detain us. Another question we really cannot answer is which of the three possibilities proposed earlier best explains the association between religiousness and the female sex. Data has long indicated that more women than men are churchgoers, so the association must be in part a cultural given. On the other hand, we have found that looking at female psychological characteristics as determinants of religious orientations provides plausible explanations for the phenomena reported in the present study.

Perhaps the best we can do is rule out the possibility that the *sole* determinants of sex differences in religiosity are the psychological characteristics of male and female.

Summary

We have in this chapter presented the ways in which fifty males and fifty females differ in their orientation toward the Catholic Church. Females were found to be more religious: they were less likely to leave the Church; they were more orthodox in their beliefs and more orthodox in their conception of the Church's beliefs. In trying to account for these religious differences, we marshalled in related evidence on psychological differences between the sexes and began to use phrases like "is due to," "is an effect of," or conversely, "determines," or "is responsible for." We began, in other words, to make inferences of causality, saying not only that X is associated with Y, but that X leads to Y. These inferences were made in the context of sex differences, but many of the explanations could apply to In-Out differences as well. If dependency, conformity, the need for affiliation, anxiety, and cognitive style are partial mediators of sex differences in religious orientation, could they not help as well to explain membership differences? More traces of causal inference will appear as the search for why is pressed into the area of parent-child interaction, and the question of causality will be faced squarely in the chapter subsequent to that.

EIGHT

Parents

As they recollect it, and as measured by the overt indices described in the first chapter, Ins and Outs had parallel histories of Catholic experience. With one exception, they were all baptized into the Church shortly after birth. The vast majority of them attended Catholic elementary schools, secondary schools, and colleges, and about half of each group had an extended period of voluntary attendance at daily Mass. It is logical to assume that the parents of these people were largely responsible for these early sets of behaviors in their children. Hence, if the early religious behavior of the two groups is identical, or at least nearly so, we can expect that the parents of both groups are very much alike.

They are alike in respects reported upon previously: practically all of them were born in the United States; most received at least a high school education; most fathers were white-collar workers and most mothers housewives. The family incomes, as remembered by subjects, were between $5,000 and $10,000. There were about three children in each family. On all these demographic variables relating to parents, there is little discrepancy between Ins and Outs.

Against this backdrop of similarities, we explore in the present chapter ways in which the parents of Ins differ from the parents of Outs. What follows is based upon subject portrayals of their parents and the parent-child relationships they experienced.

Their Parents' Catholicism

In the case of twenty-two people who were interviewed, one or both parents was not a practicing Catholic (Table 8.1). Fourteen times, it was the father who was not the practicing Catholic; six times, it was both the father and the mother; and twice it was the mother alone. In no instance was a Catholic but not practicing mother married to a husband who was Catholic and practicing. In the two cases involving mothers alone, the mother was not Catholic; and in the three instances in which the mother was Catholic but did not practice, the father was not a Catholic.

There are, on the other hand, six examples of a father who was Catholic but not practicing, and who was married to a practicing Catholic mother. Thus, even the parents of subjects bear out the sex differences uncovered previously: females are more likely to remain in the Church; and when there is an influence between the sexes regarding the Church, it is from male to female. There are no cases in which a mother gave up practice without the father already having done so, but there are six instances of the reverse.

The major association between parents' Catholicism and the current status of their children is shown in Table 8.1. There is a strong tendency for children of marriages in which one party was not a practicing Catholic to face in adulthood the ambiguity presented by the Church and define themselves as out. Of the five Ins who are exceptions to a perfect association between these two variables, four are females, and females are less likely to leave the Church. Of the seventeen

Table 8.1. In-Out Differences in Accounts of Their Parents' Catholicism

Parent not Catholic	Ins (N)	Outs (N)	χ^2 or F, p
(1) Mother	1	1	
(2) Father	3	8	
(3) Both	0	0	
Parent Catholic, but not practicing[a]			
(1) Mother	1	2	
(2) Father	1	5	
(3) Both	0	3	
Summary			
(1) Both parents practicing Catholics	45	33	$\chi^2 = 7.05$
(2) One or both parents not practicing Catholic(s)	5	17	$df = 1$ $p < .01$
Orthodoxy of practicing Catholic parent's(s') beliefs, as estimated by subject[b]	+2.33	+2.08	$F = 2.67$ $p < .1054$

[a] The criterion for "practicing Catholic" was attendance at Sunday Mass 90 per cent of the time.

[b] Subject estimated the thinking of his practicing Catholic parent(s) on the twenty items of belief; the above represents the average reply given to the twenty items.

Outs whose parents were not both practicing Catholics, eight are male and nine female. There seems to be no evidence to support the hypothesis made in the previous chapter that the association between parents' Catholicism and the status of their offspring is stronger for females.

It makes little difference to the overall association between parents' Catholicism and the current status of their offspring whether a parent was simply not Catholic or Catholic but not practicing. Nor does it appear to matter whether the parent who was not a practicing Catholic was of the same or opposite sex as the subject, although there are not enough cases of a nonpracticing Catholic mother to insure a sound testing of this hypothesis.

There is a disparity, though not a statistically significant one, in the orthodoxy of parents as estimated by the subjects. The procedure for estimation involved the subjects' going through the now familiar list of twenty beliefs and indicating what he felt was "the thinking of your parents on these matters." If, as in most cases, both parents were practicing Catholics, the subject averaged his reply for the two of them (usually they weren't very discrepant). If only one parent was a practicing Catholic, the subject responded for him or her alone. If neither was a practicing Catholic, the subject answered for the one nominally Catholic. The orthodoxy-of-parents score is the average reply given to these twenty belief-formulas. Looking at these scores, we see that the practicing Catholic parents of Ins are felt to be slightly more orthodox in their present thinking than the practicing Catholic parents of Outs.

Although this average difference is not statistically significant, there are significant differences on four individual items: parents of Ins are reported to be more accepting of the beliefs having to do with Christ's resurrection (Item 5), immortality (Item 6), missing Sunday Mass (Item 8), and contraception (Item 20). These differences do not appear to represent projections of subjects' own beliefs, because sex differences do not appear in these estimates of parents' beliefs, while status differences do. What the differences probably mean is that the practicing Catholic parents of Outs actually are somewhat less orthodox than those of Ins, this due in some instances to the presence of a nonpracticing Catholic spouse.

A diagram summarizing the positions of self, Church, and parent on belief orthodoxy is shown in Figure 8.1. Outs, of course, are much less orthodox than Ins; their practicing Catholic parent(s) is (are) slightly less orthodox than those of Ins; and the Church they perceive is more orthodox than

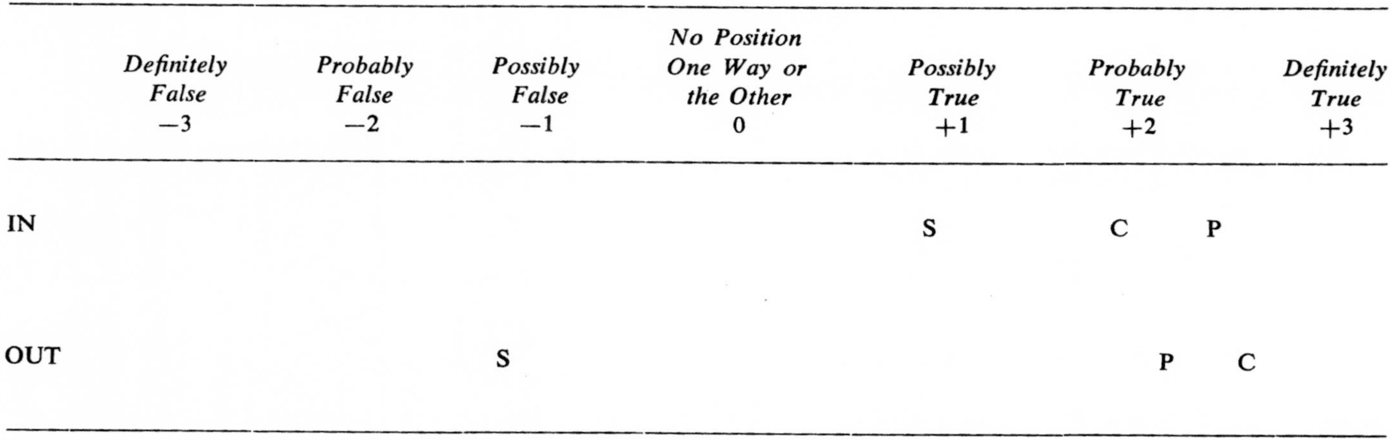

	Definitely False −3	Probably False −2	Possibly False −1	No Position One Way or the Other 0	Possibly True +1	Probably True +2	Definitely True +3
IN					S	C P	
OUT			S			P	C

Figure 8.1. In-Out differences in the orthodoxy of their own beliefs (S), in their estimation of the orthodoxy of the Church's beliefs (C), and in their estimation of the orthodoxy of their parents' beliefs (P). Each case is averaged for the twenty belief items. For the full wording of each belief item, see Figure 6.2.

that of Ins. The In-Out reversal of the Church and the parent positions in Figure 8.1 is interesting. Presumably, orthodox parents create children who wish to remain in the Church; but in order to remain in, their adult sons and daughters must redefine the Church, making it less orthodox and more compatible with what they themselves believe. In the generation between parent and child, then, the meaning and importance of orthodoxy has shifted, being beforehand a mark of loyalty and afterwards something distinct from loyalty.

Other Characteristics of Their Parents

Direct discussion of the respondents' parents began with four open-ended questions asking subjects to say what they especially liked or admired about each parent and what in particular they disliked or found not admirable. They then answered questions about closeness to each parent, parental discipline, parental absence, and then responded to a series of adjective pairs descriptive of each parent.

As far as the open-ended questions go (Table 8.2), there is a tendency for mothers of male and female Ins to be liked or admired for virtues such as love, goodness, selflessness, and warmth, and mothers of male and female Outs to be liked or admired for "harder" virtues such as patience, perseverance, devotion, dedication as a mother, and competence. There is no similar distinction between In and Out descriptions of their fathers, although in a previous section of the questionnaire more male and female Ins (fifteen) than male and female Outs (six) included their father among the people they admired most. Thus, Ins seem to have stronger positive ties to their home than have Outs.

There is also a tendency for those families with instances of divorce, separation, abandonment, or alcoholism to have children who currently consider themselves out of the Church. Likewise, those subjects who express a basic antipathy toward

Table 8.2. In-Out Differences in Open-Ended Descriptions of Their Parents

	Ins (N)	Outs (N)	χ^2, df, p
Quality liked or admired in mother			
(1) "Love" or equivalent[a]	30	15	$\chi^2 = 7.92$
(2) Other	20	35	$df = 1$
			$p < .005$
Quality liked or admired in father			
(1) "Love" or equivalent	14	8	$\chi^2 = 1.46$
(2) Other	36	42	$df = 1$
			N.S.
(A) Divorce, separation, abandonment of home, or alcoholism attributed to parent(s)	1	6	
(B) Basic antipathy expressed toward parent(s), not included in (A)[b]	2	5	$\chi^2 = 5.60$ $df = 2$
(C) Neither (A) nor (B)	47	39	N.S.
Summary (Table 8.1 and above)			
(1) Both parents practicing Catholics and neither (A) nor (B) above	43	26	
(2) One or both parents not practicing Catholics and/or (A) or (B) above	7	24	$\chi^2 = 11.97$ $df = 1$ $p < .001$

Note: See Appendix II, p. 252, Questions 13–16. Replies to these questions were coded independently and blindly by three judges, all three agreeing 90.5 per cent of the time. Cases disagreed upon were placed in those categories two of the judges had agreed upon.

[a] e.g., "Goodness," "Selflessness," "Warmth," "Sensitivity"

[b] e.g., "mother an evil, shrewish bitch—gave love as an investment," "father and I don't get along"

one or both of their parents are more likely to be Outs. Absence of a parent from the home is not in itself associated with the current status of the offspring.

Assembling the results of this section with those of the one preceding leads to the summary table at the bottom of Table 8.2. Of the sixty-nine sets of parents in which both parents practiced Catholicism and about which there is no report of divorce, etc., nor any expression of basic negative feeling, forty-three have an adult son or daughter who currently defines himself or herself as in the Church and twenty-six have a son or daughter who currently defines himself or herself as out. Of the thirty-one sets of parents who do not meet the above conditions, seven have an offspring who is in and twenty-four have one who is out. This association is highly significant.

The Exceptions: Seven Ins

Of equal importance are the exceptions to the association. Is there anything unique about their experience of Catholicism or their present position with respect to it that sets them off from the majority who create the association?

Among Ins, the first exception is a male whose father left home for several years and later divorced his wife. The father was not Catholic and was antagonistic toward the Church. The mother was Catholic but did not practice, and was not herself favorably disposed toward the Church. Although baptized at birth, the subject did not attend a Catholic elementary or secondary school. He did, however, attend a Catholic college and became close to several priests there. Through their influence he underwent what he termed "a conversion." It affected him so profoundly that he entered a Catholic seminary at the end of his freshman year. Ten years later, he gave up studying for the priesthood, but he still attends Mass about once a month and considers himself within the Church. No other subject reported anything similar to this conversion experience.

A second male In expressed basic negative feelings toward both his mother and father, each of whom was a practicing Catholic. By any number of measures, he is the most "out" of the male Ins: he is the least orthodox of all Ins in belief, more rejecting of the twenty beliefs than thirty of the Outs; he attends Mass perhaps twice a year and confesses never; he is the only In to split the Church into two parts and say that he does not belong to the institutional part. His Church, in fact, is the least orthodox and most liberal of all In Churches because it is a reflection of himself. Most of his friends are not Catholic—indeed, he was suggested as a potential Out interviewee by two separate sources. In his own mind, however, he is clearly in: "To say I am out would concede that a narrow definition of In-ness is true. I don't want that definition to be true."

The third male exception said he had little admiration for his distant, apathetic father. Both his parents were devout Catholics. The position of this subject is also very close to the borderline: he is second only to the above subject in belief unorthodoxy; his Church is the second most unorthodox in belief and is among the most liberal of those described by Ins. He has the third lowest ΣVI score, indicating positive feeling toward membership (Chapter 5), and he has the highest ambivalence score ($\Sigma|VI| - |\Sigma VI|$) of all the subjects. Yet he is very relaxed about his position in the Church: "I define it in such a way that doctrinal problems are meaningless. I would give up Catholicism if the Church insisted on defining itself in a way to exclude people like me."

Of the four female Ins who are exceptions to the general association indicated in Table 8.2, the first had a mother who was not Catholic. This subject is the only one of those who responded to a follow-up questionnaire (Chapter 10) to say she had subsequently changed status and left the Church. "Left the Church," however, is not an adequate description. She wrote:

"Catholic" has become merely a word, a title, not an indication of what I believe. I am lying when I tell people I am Catholic. I have always been taught this in the Catholic college I attended, that a person must adhere to what he really believes, and that if he finds something no longer within his belief, he is obliged to end his allegiance and adhere to his new beliefs. I have trouble applying this rule to myself but I think I must do it.

Somewhere in what I have said must lie the reason for my change of status, I'm not sure. I think maybe my status has not changed, I have just named it correctly this time. I still attend Mass, however sporadically. I have found nothing new to adhere to, but I am looking. Perhaps some day I'll call myself a "new" Catholic or a "reformed" Catholic, or maybe nothing at all.

Another female subject came from a family that was not Catholic but that gave the children a chance to choose a religion when it came time for college. Her older brother chose a Catholic college and converted to Catholicism. Subsequently, the mother of the family became Catholic, the subject herself chose a Catholic college and converted, the father and a younger brother both became Catholic. From the beginning, the family had been religious but not attached to any one denomination. They all ended up being Catholic.

The father of the third female exception was not a Catholic. In belief, this subject is the second most unorthodox female In, and she is the most liberal about the future of the Church. Her Church is the most unorthodox in belief of those described by the female Ins and is also among the most liberal. She frequently chooses to remain in the Church, although there has been "no decision for the rest of my life. . . . I feel a tension and ambiguity," she said, "in disagreeing with so much of the structure and calling myself a member. I haven't solved the tension yet."

The final exception is a female whose father was Catholic but did not practice. She is of average orthodoxy in belief, as is the Church whose thinking she estimates. But her ΣVI score is the third lowest of the female Ins and her ambivalence-toward-membership score is the greatest.

Of these seven exceptions, then, two experienced conversions of one kind or another (no other subject did), four are among those Ins closest to the borderline on a number of measures, and one has subsequently crossed the border and defined herself as out of the Church.

The Exceptions: Twenty-Six Outs

When looking at In exceptions to the general association, we saw how their experience of Catholicism or their present position with respect to it differed from that of other Ins. There is little difference between the Out exceptions and other Outs, however, in their experience of Catholicism or their present position with respect to it, at least as far as can be told by inspecting several key measures. Both sets of Outs are equally rejecting of Catholic beliefs, and their Church is equally orthodox in belief and conservative on other issues.

Hence, we will take the approach of analyzing in a more refined way the parents of these Outs, doing so by dropping from the analysis those thirty-one subjects (twenty-four Outs and seven Ins) whose parents were not both practicing Catholics, or divorced, etc., or evocative of basic antipathy from their offspring. We will compare the twenty-six Outs who are left with the remaining forty-three Ins on more quantified measures of (a) their parents' Catholicism and (b) other characteristics of their parents.

THEIR PARENTS' CATHOLICISM

Three of the Outs retained in this analysis indicated that, while both parents practiced Catholicism up until the time the subject entered college, they have either stopped practicing or have become much more hostile toward Catholicism. None of the In subjects reported this. This shift in parent attitudes may be a result of the shift in their child's feelings toward the Church and/or it might mean their underlying feeling toward Catholicism was not thoroughly positive all along.

There is a tendency for the parents of the male Ins retained in this analysis to be thought of as more orthodox and conservative than the parents of the male Outs who are retained, but the difference is short of statistical significance. This disparity may mean the parents of male Outs became less orthodox as their son grew up; it may also reflect the effect of the Out son's shift upon his parents' present thinking; or it may simply be a case of the subject's projecting his own beliefs onto those of his parents.

Other than these slight effects we find no difference in the Catholicism of the parents of these sixty-nine subjects. Generally, they are equally orthodox and conservative, practice to the same degree, and appear equally favorable toward the Catholic Church.

OTHER CHARACTERISTICS OF THEIR PARENTS

Each subject in this study characterized his parents on ten pairs of adjectives and indicated which parent was more responsible for disciplining him and which he felt closer to while in the home. For the sixty-nine subjects presently under consideration, significant In-Out differences for one or both of the sexes were discovered for those variables listed in Figure 8.2 (males), Figure 8.3 (females), and Table 8.3 (both).

That adjectives descriptive of the mother show greater differences than those descriptive of the father is caused by the fact that most of the subjects excluded from the present analysis were dropped because of characteristics attributed to the father. Eighteen of the thirty-one were dropped because of the father, eight because of both father and mother, and only five because of the mother alone. The effect of analyzing only sixty-nine subjects is to heighten differences descriptive of mothers and to lower differences descriptive of fathers. When looking only at the sixty-nine subjects, fathers appear to be more attractive than when looking at all one hundred.

For the thirty-six females retained in this analysis, the WARM-COLD variable used to characterize the mother proves to be a good In-Out discriminant. This variable has been found to be of major importance in other social psycho-

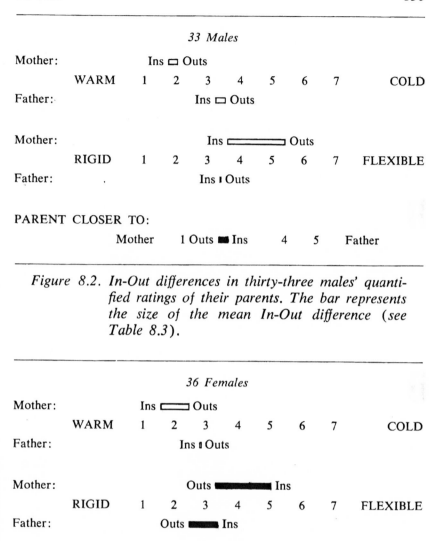

Figure 8.2. In-Out differences in thirty-three males' quantified ratings of their parents. The bar represents the size of the mean In-Out difference (see Table 8.3).

Figure 8.3. In-Out differences in thirty-six females' quantified ratings of their parents. The bar represents the size of the mean In-Out difference (see Table 8.3).

Table 8.3. In-Out Differences in Sixty-Nine Subjects' Quantified Ratings of Their Parents

	Males (N = 33)				
Variable	Mean Ins (N = 22)	Mean Outs (N = 11)	Mean In-Out Diff.	t	p < (2-tailed)
Mother WARM-COLD	1.77	2.00	− .23	.48	N.S.
Father WARM-COLD	3.23	3.64	− .41	.69	N.S.
Mother RIGID-FLEXIBLE	3.55	5.45	−1.90	3.44	.002
Father RIGID-FLEXIBLE	3.36	3.36	0.00	0.00	N.S.
PARENT CLOSER TO (Mother-Father)	2.23	1.91	.32	.63	N.S.

	Females (N = 36)				
Variable	Mean Ins (N = 21)	Mean Outs (N = 15)	Mean In-Out Diff.	t	p < (2-tailed)
Mother WARM-COLD	1.57	2.47	− .90	2.36	.05
Father WARM-COLD	2.85	2.87	− .02	.03	N.S.
Mother RIGID-FLEXIBLE	5.00	3.40	1.60	2.48	.02
Father RIGID-FLEXIBLE	3.45	2.60	.85	1.49	N.S.
PARENT CLOSER TO (Mother-Father)	1.62	2.73	−1.11	2.15	.05

Analysis of Variance: Significant Effects			
Variable	Effect	F	p <
Mother WARM-COLD	Status (In-Out)	3.93	.0516
Mother RIGID-FLEXIBLE	Status X Sex	16.48	.0002
PARENT CLOSER TO (Mother-Father)	Status X Sex	3.84	.0545

logical research involving the perception of people (Asch, 1946; Kelley, 1950). While all the present subjects tend to rate their mother as warm, female Ins consider their mothers significantly warmer than do female Outs. Male Ins feel their mothers were warmer than do male Outs, but the difference is not statistically significant. For both sexes, status of subjects separates responses on this variable with $p < .0516$.

This difference is not as apparent when all one hundred subjects are included in the analysis, although the In-Out difference is in the same direction. More Ins than Outs, it was reported earlier, stated that "love" or its equivalent was a quality they admired in their mother (Table 8.2).

Fathers are rated midway between warm and cold by all subjects, with females, regardless of their status, thinking of them as warmer than do males (69 Ss' analysis: $F = 1.99$, $p < .1630$; 100 Ss' analysis: $F = 7.33$, $p < .0081$).

Differences in the perception of the mother also come out on the DISTANT-CLOSE variable, female Ins describing their mothers as closer than female Outs. The same, to a lesser degree, is true of male Ins. The differences, however, are not significant at the .05 level.

Another variable that turns out to discriminate significantly between Ins and Outs is the RIGID-FLEXIBLE variable as applied to the mother. Male Outs see their mothers as more flexible than male Ins, who regard their mothers as midway between rigid and flexible. The reverse applies to females: Ins feel their mothers were more flexible than do Outs, who see their mothers as having been halfway between the two extremes. For the sixty-nine subjects, this interaction effect is significant at the .0002 level and for all one hundred at the .0016 level. The same effect is also seen in a less obvious way on the LAX CONSCIENCE-SCRUPULOUS CONSCIENCE variable.

The fathers of In and Out males on the RIGID-FLEXIBLE variable have the same score, while fathers of female Outs are rated more rigid, but not significantly so, than those of female Ins.

The final observation has to do with replies to the question, "Which parent did you feel closer to while you were in the home?" The usual answer is the subject's mother, this no doubt being related to the fact that she was in the home most of the day while the father was not. It is also connected with the father's being absent for lengthier periods of time, often in connection with his employment. Twenty-four fathers, as compared with only five mothers, are reported to have been absent from the home "for a considerable period of time."

Once the general inclination to respond "mother" is taken into account, however, we find that Ins tended to feel closer to the parent of the same sex and Outs to the parent of the opposite sex. This interaction effect for the sixty-nine subjects is significant with $p < .0545$. When all one hundred subjects are analyzed, it is significant with $p < .0320$.

This difference in reported closeness to either parent is not a function of one group's mother or father being physically present in the home more than another's. Cases of the father's absence were identical for male Ins and Outs (seven each) and for female Ins and Outs (five each), and the distribution of the five cases of the mother's absence works against the hypothesis of a connection between physical and psychological closeness. The reported difference in closeness, then, must be entirely a psychological one.

Other evidence that differential closeness is not related to actual presence in the home is that, in stating which parent was more responsible for discipline, In and Out subjects of either sex showed no significant differences. The one slight difference that occurs is that, among the thirty-three males retained for this analysis, the Outs tend to say the father disciplined while Ins say both parents did.

Differential closeness to one parent rather than to the other also appears to be independent of what might be termed absolute closeness. The twenty-one female Ins rate both mother and father closer than do the fifteen female Outs; yet, when asked which of the two parents they were closer to, female

Outs feel more of a pull toward the father. The thirty-three male Ins and Outs rate their fathers equally close; the Ins rate their mothers slightly closer; but, when choosing between parents, male Outs are closer to the mother than the father and male Ins experience more of a pull toward the father. For these sixty-nine subjects, the correlation between closeness to mother and differential closeness to either parent is −.161, and the correlation between closeness to father and differential closeness to either parent is +.418. In brief, Ins, more than Outs, say they were (1) closer to both parents and (2) differentially closer to the parent of the same sex.

Another way to present the data for these sixty-nine subjects and to give an idea of the magnitude of the In-Out differences is to use frequency counts. For males, a translation of the Mother RIGID-FLEXIBLE variable would read: ten of eleven Outs (91 per cent) said their mother was on the flexible side (rating of 5, 6, or 7), whereas only six of twenty-two Ins (27 per cent) did. One Out (9 per cent), compared with nine Ins (41 per cent) had a combination of a father whom they felt as close or closer to than the mother (rating of 3, 4, or 5) and a mother described as rigid or at least not flexible (rating of 1, 2, 3, or 4).

For females, the most discriminating question that could be asked is: Was the mother described as very warm (rating of 1 or 2), flexible (rating of 5, 6, or 7), and was the subject closer to her mother (rating of 1 or 2)? Twelve of twenty-one Ins (57 per cent) say "Yes," while only two of fifteen Outs (31 per cent) do.

It should be noted that no significant association is evident between the present status of a subject of either sex and his or her description of a parent as moody or even-tempered, dominant or submissive, sympathetic or unsympathetic, mild or harsh, naive or sophisticated, out for his own or the subject's good, and intelligent or not intelligent in religious matters, either in the analysis of the sixty-nine or of the one hundred subjects.

It becomes clear that the twenty-six Out exceptions to the summary association in Table 8.2 cannot all be adequately discriminated from Ins on these quantified descriptions of their parents. A fair number of them appear to be very similar to Ins in depicting their parents and their parents' Catholicism. Relationships with one's parents can only be one of many factors affecting a person's current status with respect to the Church, although it is certainly one of the most important and may even be the most important.

Related Evidence and Hints of Explanation

Rather simple concepts of identification with parental standards and cognitive consistency between self and parent can explain the major association between parents' Catholicism and the present status of their offspring (Table 8.1). They can also account for the relation between the expression of basic antipathy toward a parent and the subject's current status (Table 8.2). What we should concentrate on, then, in ferreting out evidence related to our own, is explaining In-Out differences in perception of parents among those sixty-nine subjects both of whose parents are practicing Catholics and who evoke no serious expression of antipathy from their offspring.

The basic question to be asked about these subjects is: Why are certain parental characteristics seemingly conducive to the adoption and permanent internalization by their children of a value espoused by the parent, the value in this case being a desire to be a member of the Catholic Church? Because certain subjects have been dropped from the analysis, the question is asked with controls built in for the amount of Catholic education and the extent of religious practice shown by the child, the Catholicism of the parent, and any basic antipathy expressed toward the parent.

Relevant to our question are studies of imitative behavior in young children. Many of these have confirmed that an adult model who is warm and nurturant is more likely to evoke imitative behavior than one who is not. In a typical example (Bandura and Huston, 1961), a female model spends two play sessions with a preschool child. During these sessions she is warm, attentive, and helpful with half the children and distant and aloof with the others. Later, in a testing session that is staged as a game, more of her incidental behavior (e.g., saying "Here I go" or "March, march, march") is imitated by the children who had been in the warm, nurturant play sessions. Bandura draws no distinction between this imitative behavior and learning by "identification."

There also is evidence that the greater a model's social power—defined as his ability to control resources important to the subject—the greater his imitability (Bandura et al., 1963; Grusec and Mischel, 1966). Another theorist suggests that models are copied because of envy for the privileged status they hold (Whiting, 1960). Evidence is mixed on whether a model of the same sex or of the opposite sex elicits greater imitation in young children (Baldwin, 1967, p. 43; Mischel, 1966). In one experiment, both boys and girls imitated a male adult when he had greater control over resources and a female adult when she had the power (Bandura et al., 1963).

In a recent review of the research on conscience formation (Hoffman, 1963), moral orientations based on fear of external detection and punishment were found to be associated with "power assertive discipline" on the part of the parent, i.e., with the use of physical punishment and mental deprivation. On the other hand, moral orientations characterized by independence of external sanctions and high guilt were related to "nonpower assertive discipline," this being the use of psychological or love-oriented techniques. The association between love-oriented discipline and greater internalization of moral values has been found in retrospective reports of male adults (MacKinnon, 1938) and in mothers' accounts of their children (Sears et al., 1957), and the relation between physical punishment and lack of conscience in studies of juvenile delinquents (McCord and McCord, 1956).

Adoption and internalization of a parent's moral values, then, seems to take place in an atmosphere of love and warmth, not in an atmosphere of power and physical punishment. Love and its withdrawal do not in themselves appear to be the key causal factors in the formation of a fully developed conscience; rather, atmospheres of love and warmth usually occasion more effective procedures such as pointing out how a transgression hurts the parent or others. Same-sex and cross-sex interactions between parent and child have yet to be reliable predictors of differences in moral orientations, with maternal disciplinary practices alone being the better indicators (Hoffman and Saltzstein, 1967). There is some evidence below, however, that a son's incorporation of parental standards increases as his identification with his father grows.

More thorough observation of cross-sex and same-sex parent-child interaction has been done in other studies of parent identification. At this point, the data on boys indicates a clear shift from preference for the mother to preference for the father and that on girls shows a general but more ambiguous tendency to prefer the mother as a model throughout childhood (Kohlberg, 1966).

Because the very young boy is not aware of sex differences, it seems reasonable to consider his early mother orientation non-sex-typed. Fairly consistent categorization of himself and others on the basis of sex does not begin before three and a constant gender identity based on awareness of anatomical differences is not established until around seven. The desire to imitate a male adult model seems to begin around four or five, and preference for depending upon a male adult can be seen at age six. Contrary to Freud's postulation of a rather sudden and total incorporation of paternal values in response to a real or fantasized threat of castration, identification with the father appears to be facilitated not by fear but by paternal warmth. It has also been shown that the competence, power, and prestige shown by the father is conducive to his being identified with by his son (Kohlberg, 1966).

Whether paternal warmth and power are causes of greater identification or effects of it is an unresolved question. Whether the learning of sex-appropriate behaviors is an antecedent condition of father identification or a consequence of it is also disputed. But there is at least consistency in the finding of correlations linking together imitation of the father, perception of similarity between self and the father, preference for masculine values, and affectional attitudes toward the father, including an attitude of affectional dependency (Kohlberg, 1966). Several studies also indicate that internalized moral judgments increase in the same years that father identification is rising and actually find positive correlations between measures of father-identification and measures of acceptance of the conventional moral code (Kohlberg, 1963, 1964).

There are a number of complicating factors in understanding data on parent identification in girls: there is no shift from one parent to another as there is in boys; both boys and girls begin around the age of four or five to be aware of the greater power attached to the male role and so are more likely to prefer it, and it may be the case that the complementary role of the parent of the opposite sex is more important in girls than in boys. In any case, girls still prefer the parent of the same sex throughout childhood, though the preference is not as clear-cut as that of boys for their father. Maternal warmth, too, appears related to identification with the mother, though again the evidence is mixed (Kohlberg, 1966).

The consistent findings in all this research are that parental warmth leads to the adoption of the parents' behavior and values, that parental power (when not punishing) has the same effect, and that both sexes end up preferring the parent of the same sex as a model to identify with. Our data fits in nicely with these findings, with the exception that we pick up no associations on variables that could be interpreted as revealing parental power.

Looking at the data for the thirty-six females, we see that those mothers who are described as having been warm and flexible, and to whom their daughters were relatively closer, have daughters who face the ambiguous borderline around the Catholic Church and define themselves as in. Presumably, a value more deeply internalized because of greater parental warmth and higher identification with the parent of the same sex makes them perceive the ambiguity in a certain way and take their position accordingly. It must be remembered that the females under discussion are equated for the Catholicism of the parents, for lack of gross disturbance in the family, amount of Catholic education, and extent of early religious practice.

The data for the thirty-three males is more puzzling because the only significant discriminant is the Mother RIGID-FLEXIBLE variable, and no other research suggests that the rigidity or flexibility of the parent of the opposite sex in itself brings about a greater internalization of parental values. We could hypothesize that the greater rigidity of the male In mothers creates rigid sons who are less willing to change and leave the Church. There are a number of problems with this hypothesis, however: (1) we do not know whether greater rigidity in a person leads to leaving the Church or remaining in it, since staying in often involves more complex cognitive reorganization than leaving; (2) among females, greater rigidity on the part of a parent is associated with the daughter's being out of the Church; (3) the male In was relatively closer to the father than the average subject—how could he then have identified primarily with the mother and have adopted her rigidity?

Perhaps maternal rigidity or flexibility works in conjunction with some other factor to make for a more lasting adoption of a value. An explanation in this direction is suggested by a study on the development of achievement motivation in young boys (Rosen and D'Andrade, 1959). This research found that the combination of an affectionate mother who dominated her son during various experimental tasks and a father who was competent but tended to let his son work on his own during the tasks was associated with the son's being more achievement oriented. Dominance and greater involvement on the part of the mother was not only tolerable but helpful, but had it come from the rival father, the authors suggested, it would have been perceived as a competitive threat and would have crushed the boy. Analogously, perhaps greater rigidity in the mother leads to a greater internalization of parental values if it comes in conjunction with and does not obstruct other important factors such as warmth on the part of both parents and high identification with the parent of the same sex.

There were nine male Ins (41 per cent) and only one male Out (9 per cent) who both (1) felt as close or closer to the father than to the mother and (2) had a mother who was rigid, or at least not on the flexible side. This particular combination of parent-child interaction may be conducive to a more permanent internalization in the son of a value espoused by both parents. This value, this want, so our explanation has run, is a determining agent of how a son defines himself when faced with the ambiguity of the Catholic Church.

Summary

The present chapter has searched for ways in which the parents of Ins differ from the parents of Outs. A gross analysis showed that Ins were much more likely to come from families in which both parents were practicing Catholics, in which there was no incidence of divorce, separation, abandonment, or alcoholism, and in which no basic antipathy was created between parent and child. A microscopic analysis revealed that, of all the subjects whose families fit the above description, Ins tended to feel closer to the parent of the same sex and Outs to the parent of the opposite sex, the effect being stronger for females than males. From this and other data, it appears that, when the Catholicism of the parent and gross disturbance in the family are controlled, family warmth and identification with a warm, flexible mother leads to a daughter's more permanent internalization of the desire to be a Catholic. With the same controls, family warmth, identification with the father, and a moderate amount of rigidity in the mother leads to a greater internalization of the same desire in the son. "Degree of internalization" seems to be a key concept in explaining why the ambiguity of the Catholic Church is perceived as it is.

NINE

An Explanation

In those chapters covering "The Results of Change," one's self-determined status of being in or out of the Catholic Church was related to his religious beliefs, especially those about the other world, to his assessment of the role of membership in aiding the attainment of values, and to his overall understanding of the Catholic Church. Clear and generally dichotomous stands were taken by Ins and Outs in all areas involving the perception of ambiguity, despite the fact that both groups' early experience of Catholicism appeared to have been similar. In going through a critical period of change before reaching their present position, too, Ins and Outs placed similar information in radically different contexts, Ins viewing negative elements in the Church as accidental to their basic conception of it and able to be changed, Outs seeing the same elements as central to the Church and unalterable in the foreseeable future. It seemed that some a-rational or prerational starting point was determining how information about the Catholic Church was perceived and structured.

What remains on the agenda is to take the data presented in these chapters and the two subsequent ones on sex differences and parent-child relationships and construct an explanation of that a-rational starting point that leads In and Out perceptions to go in opposite directions. The task is one of inference, of making the most reasonable estimate of the source, direction, and endpoint of the causal flow between variables. All that the data contains in itself is a number of differences between Ins and Outs or, put another way, a number of associations between In-Out status and beliefs, values, perceptions of the Church, and descriptions of parents. An association between two variables does not in itself indicate which of the pair determines the other or whether both are determined by some third variable. If X and Y are related, we do not know whether X causes Y, Y causes X, or both are caused by Z. Does belief in the resurrection of Christ determine one's In-Out status, does one's status determine his assent to that belief, or does something else determine both? The kind of data that we have—from an interview at one point in time—does not enable us to make a definitive judgment of the direction of causality.

Certain criteria, however, can be used to make a reasonable estimate of the major cause variables and the major effect variables. For one thing, if X causes Y, it must occur before Y and be able to exert influence on Y. Sex and position on Belief Item 3 ("There is a God."), for example, are related; sex and most of its associated characteristics, however, were fixed long before the present position on the belief item was taken. One can thus imagine sex effecting a change in the belief, but not the belief effecting a change in one's sex. Nor can there be some third variable that influences both the sex of a person and his belief. We can conclude, then, that sex is a determining agent of the belief.

Variables that point to pervasive and long term relationships can also be thought of as more influential than ones that do not. Thus, while both present income and descriptions of parents are related to subjects' current status, the relationship referred to in the description of the parents (especially where the description is of overt activity such as practicing Catholicism) is probably more a determining agent of status than is present income. Again, a parent's practice of Catholicism in the past may affect his child's current status, but the child's status cannot affect the parent's past practice of Catholicism.

Thus, in piecing together an explanation of the starting point that shapes one's perception of the ambiguous Catholic Church and the positioning of himself with respect to it, I have considered cause variables those that refer back farthest in time, point to long term relationships, and appear able to exert influence on other, less important variables, which are then designated effect variables.

Of the cause variables, the most important ones are those referring to the parents of subjects, and the evidence assembled in Chapter 8 leads to the conclusion that, because of particular parent-child relationships, some subjects internalized the desire to be a member of the Catholic Church more deeply than others. Those whose parents were not both practicing Catholics, our explanation runs, internalized such a desire less securely because of the inconsistency involved in seeing one model attend Church while the other did not. Or, when both models consistently practiced Catholicism, some were not identified with because of gross disturbance in the home: divorce, separation, abandonment, alcoholism. Finally, even in those homes in which both parents practiced Catholicism, and in which there was no gross disturbance, we find that among females family warmth and identification with a warm, flexible mother produced more internalization of parental values and that among males family warmth, identification with the father, and a moderate amount of rigidity in the mother had the same effect. In the case of both female and male, this greater internalization led to a more permanent desire to be a member of the Church.

What we are saying, then, is that, even though two sets of people attended Mass and the Sacraments with the same frequency during childhood and adolescence, even though each received the same amount of Catholic education and by all outward signs was as Catholic as the other, one had internalized the value of being a member of the Catholic Church in a warmer, more secure, more comfortable manner than the other. This deeper internalization, the major part of an a-rational "pull" or "starting point," leads its possessors to perceive the changing Catholic Church and its possibilities in an optimistic fashion. Wanting to be members of the Church, but faced with an unattractive Church, they split the Church into visible and invisible elements and identify with the latter. The cognitive effort of redefinition is worthwhile because the positive value of membership is preserved.

Those with shallower internalizations of the desire to be Catholic, despite all the outward Catholic education and practice of their religion, find it more compatible simply to abandon the Church when it becomes unattractive. In some instances, the internalization, being inconsistent, may have been a source of conflict and tension, and giving up membership may have been a relief. In others, the internalization might better be described as "weak" rather than "a source of conflict"; and, while leaving would bring no great relief, there still would be no reason to go through the cognitive effort of redefinition that staying in would involve.

This explanation assumes (1) that a subject's description of his parents is largely veridical and (2) that the influence passing from parent to child was substantially greater in the past than it is in the present. The first assumption is reasonable because the bulk of our explanation rests on descriptions of parents' overt behavior (their practice of Catholicism), and it is unlikely that such behavior will be misreported. There is also a trace of evidence (Chapter 8) that descriptions of parents' beliefs were not artificially affected by a subject's present status.

The second assumption should concern us more, for it is possible that a person would be reluctant to leave the Church because leaving would impair a positively valued present relationship with his parents. Those whose parents were not practicing Catholics would not so impair a relationship by leaving, nor would those who feel more distant from or experience basic antipathy toward their parents be as concerned about maintaining a positive relationship.

The parents of most subjects, however, were living at some distance from them, and many of the parents of Outs did not know their son or daughter had left the Church. When visiting their families, a number of Outs kept their status unknown by attending Mass dutifully. Those parents who would be upset by their child's leaving could be, and were, easily kept in the dark about their child's status. We cannot conclude, then, that parents' present influence has much effect on their offspring's self-defined status, and we can feel comfortable with the second assumption.

Saying that Outs had a shallower internalization of the desire to be Catholic means that we cannot say most of them left the Church because of an "authority problem" or a "generational conflict" with their parents, that their rebellion against the Church is a disguised form of a rebellion against their parents. There is generational conflict evident among both Ins and Outs (they do move away from their parents' beliefs and values), but both groups show as well adoption of their parents' beliefs and values. Many of the Outs' parents simply did not place as high a premium on Catholicism; their offspring assumed this evaluation and carried it one step further. Or, valuing membership in the Church highly, the Outs' parents did not behave toward their child in a manner conducive to his adoption of their attitude. Such a failure at secure adoption is not a rebellion against the parent.

It would be even more inaccurate to say that feelings toward the parents were "displaced" onto the Church, that one felt hostile toward the Church because he was hostile toward his parents. In the classical Freudian sense, displacement means that hostile feelings toward one party (e.g., a parent) are driven from consciousness and find their outlet by being directed to some other party (e.g., the Church). For displacement in this sense to occur, overt feelings toward the original party must be positive. The association we have, however, is between overt negative feeling expressed toward a parent (or simply a description of a parent as colder or more distant) and dissociation from the Church, not at all the classical displacement dynamic.

A second constituent of the a-rational starting point we are seeking to explain appears to derive from another cause variable, the sex of subjects. The meaning of Chapter 7 is that the cultural association between femininity and religion, probably in conjunction with such female sex characteristics as dependency, conformity, need for affiliation, anxiety, and a field dependent cognitive style leads females to take more orthodox positions on belief and be less likely to leave the Church. The internalized cultural expectation and other psychological characteristics constitute part of the "pull" or "want" that leads females to perceive the ambiguity surrounding the Catholic Church in a particular way.

A third factor having considerable bearing on a person's status, and one not discussed previously, is his immediate circle of friends. The transitions made by Ins and Outs were done not by individuals but by pairs and small groups. Females, we have seen, were often influenced by males during the period of change. That friendship patterns are related to In-Out status is also evidenced by the fact that In subjects generally suggested the names of other Ins for prospective interviews and Outs the names of other Outs (Table 2.1). During the interview itself, Ins reported that an average of about five good friends had "gone through roughly the same process" as they had and remained in the Church, while only two good friends of theirs had left. Outs, on the other hand, said that about five of their good friends had left the Church as they themselves had.[1]

We cannot ascertain, however, whether one's primary group causes him to perceive the ambiguity surrounding the Church in a certain way. Sherif (1936) has demonstrated with the autokinetic effect how we depend on others to stabilize our perception of ambiguous stimuli, and Asch (1956) has shown that the dependency is less when the stimuli used are not so ambiguous. It may be that one's group does influence him, but one may also influence his group to see as he does, or he may seek out a group that is compatible with his own views. Whatever the case, perception is done in groups, not by individuals.

We might hypothesize that the catalysts of activity toward leaving the Church in many primary groups are (1) males and (2) those whose internalization of the desire to be Catholic was less profound or a greater source of conflict in the first place. These might instigate the thought process leading females and those with more secure internalizations to follow suit and leave or to re-evaluate and stay in, finding a new primary group in the process. Males do seem to have been catalysts for females on some occasions, but we have no way of telling whether those with shallower internalizations spurred on those with deeper ones.

Many factors thought at the outset of this study to have an effect on one's status and his perception of the Catholic Church did not prove to be significant determinants. The religious figures—priests, nuns, and so on—who were associated with Catholicism during the subject's school years were one of these. Looking back, Outs regard their religious instructors in grammar and high school as less intelligent than

1. Comparing Ins and Outs on number of friends who have left the Church, $t = 4.69$ ($p < .001$, 2-tailed). Contrary to one expectation, females did not show more of this primary group effect than males.

do Ins, and they look on their college professors as having been more distant. Ins report that their religious teachers all along were more "out for my own good" than do Outs.[2] Because of the variety of instructors that these subjects must have been exposed to, however, a sounder conclusion than saying these instructors helped create the subject's present status is that these descriptions of instructors are a result of that status. More exactly, what makes these people perceive the variety within the Catholic Church in a certain way is probably the same thing that makes them perceive the variety among these religious figures in a certain way.

Because Catholicism is a fairly recent immigrant religion in the United States it was thought that one's ethnicity might be something else that relates to his starting point with respect to the Church. This did not turn out to be the case. Table 2.3 shows that In and Out subjects were quite well balanced as far as their ethnic background goes. An analysis of subjects with predominantly Irish, German, and other backgrounds on fifteen key variables turned up no effects associated with ethnicity other than that Irish and German parents were described as more orthodox, especially by Outs. Most of the present subjects were several generations removed from the immigrant experience anyway. Ninety-five per cent of their mothers and ninety-one per cent of their fathers had been born in the United States, and all of the subjects themselves were native-born United States citizens.

It was also expected that the academic field of study that subjects were engaged in might bear some relation to their perception of the Church and to their status with respect to it. Those in the physical sciences might more easily compartmentalize beliefs about science and religion and experience between the two no conflict that would prompt the re-examina-

---

2. See Appendix II, pp. 251–252, Questions 1–12. All the differences mentioned are significant at least at the .02 level, *t*-test (2-tailed).

tion of their religion. Data from physics and chemistry relates only indirectly to one's beliefs about man or God, whereas data from the social sciences could at least strike at the "Man and This World" pole of a belief system. Consideration of man in the humanities, too, or dealing with man in medicine and law might arouse inconsistencies in the belief system. Thus we hypothesized that there was less of a science–religion conflict in the physical sciences than in the social sciences or humanities. There already existed some data to back this hypothesis up: of those Catholics at the top twelve graduate schools in 1962, 89 per cent of those in the physical and biological sciences versus only 68 per cent in arts and letters attended Church weekly (Greeley, 1965).

Our data (Table 2.5) do show something of an over-representation of Outs in the humanities and of Ins in the physical and biological sciences, and I have impressions from a few subjects interviewed that compartmentalization of their science and religion did occur; but since the numbers involved are so few and some of the data runs contrary to the hypothesis, the proposition cannot be adequately confirmed, rejected, or refined here. Even if the social sciences and humanities are a pull toward leaving or unorthodoxy, the pull can hardly be as strong as the ones deriving from parent-child relationships, sex, and primary groups.

A number of strictly psychological variables could also determine the pull or push leading to one's particular perception of the Church and definition of himself as within or beyond its boundaries. From hints that appeared in the chapter on sex differences, dependency, conformity, the need for affiliation, anxiety, and a field-dependent cognitive style could all be mediators of the desire to remain a member and be orthodox. My impression from talking to one hundred subjects is that, except as related to sex, they are not; but to be certain we would need direct, independent measures of the characteristics.

One psychological characteristic that we did attempt to measure in some detail was tolerance for ambiguity, the ability to live with unresolved inconsistencies. An hypothesis prior to the collection of the data was that Ins would show more of this characteristic, since remaining in often involved a complex redefinition of membership, while leaving represented a simple end to inconsistency. Little evidence supports this expectation. On the $\Sigma|VI|-|\Sigma VI|$ score, Outs show more ambiguity in their value system with respect to membership in the Church than do Ins, but their ambiguity, no doubt, is less tension inducing since membership for them is a hypothetical state of affairs. There are no significant differences in the degree of certitude Ins and Outs show when responding to the list of twenty beliefs. In the value section of the questionnaire, there are no differences in the aspirations of Ins and Outs to stability or change, to closedness or openness, except in one case in which Outs are slightly more interested in "escaping the confines of my early background." There is nothing to suggest that Outs are less able to bear ambiguity; what inconclusive evidence there is, in fact, is in the other direction.

The lack of any conclusive findings with respect to the ability to tolerate ambiguity may be because of the concept of "tolerance for ambiguity" itself. I found subjects in both groups more or less reflective, complex, intense, crisis prone, and anxious, but not more or less tolerant of ambiguity, that is, able to stand up under inconsistency. Some were very consistent yet appeared to feel discomfort; others were inconsistent but not reflective enough to be bothered by it. The concept of tolerance for ambiguity needs rethinking itself before it can be conceived of as a mediator of the starting points that cause people to leave the Church or remain in it.

Another characteristic, a demographic one, that may be of some importance but that was not tapped in this study is whether one's background is urban or rural, a large city or small town. Rural Catholicism may be different from urban

Catholicism, more incompatible with the sophisticated, potentially contradictory information that could precipitate a crisis of change. A rural background might also produce a mind less accustomed to the complexity needed for redefinition, an hypothesis similar to that proposed by one theorist to account for the association between urban-rural backgrounds and theoretical orientations in the field of psychology. We suspect, but do not have the data to test the proposition that transitions of young Catholics from a rural to an urban environment would lead to leaving the Church.

One final avenue that could not be explored in an interview that was my first and only contact with a subject but that might relate to In-Out differences is the actual sexual behavior of subjects. On paper, in assenting to beliefs related to sex (e.g., "premarital sexual intercourse is morally wrong"), both Ins and Outs are deviators from prescribed Catholic practice. Whether their beliefs carry over into practice, whether practice produces guilt feelings that precipitate change, and which direction the guilt would lead, are all unknown but potentially important considerations.

A Summary and Beyond

Data presented in previous chapters has been assembled here into an explanation of the a-rational starting point that shapes In and Out perceptions of the Catholic Church and leads them to retain membership or give it up. The major determinant of that starting point appears to be the depth of the original internalization of the desire to be a Catholic, deriving from particular parent-child relationships; but the cultural expectations and the psychological characteristics associated with one's sex, and the influence of one's primary group appear to affect it as well. Leaving the Church, then, or remaining in it can hardly be called the result of an intellectual decision based on the careful weighing of evidence. Though detailed rational explanations often accompany leaving or staying in, to understand a person's membership status one must comprehend that preintellectual starting point giving rise to it.

If the importance of preintellectual starting points has been established in the belief complexes of young adult Catholics, might they not also be important in other belief complexes or world views? Why intellectually sophisticated people in one case accept the philosophical thrust of a Rousseau and in another of a Camus or a Nietzsche, why some should be politically radical and others conservative, each with an elaborate rationale for his position, why two people of equal intelligence with similar information at hand should disagree on a proposed course of action: all these anomalies might be understood by getting at the starting points that shape individuals' conceptions of "what it's all about." A large component of these a-rational starting points, the present data indicate, are residues from the parents' treatment of the child, the child's adoption of attitudes appropriate to his sex, and the child's later interaction with various primary groups.

This study began with the observation that the border between In and Out Catholics was obscure and, for that reason, worth studying. As we near the study's end, we find the border no longer so ambiguous. Empirically, a number of things distinguish Ins and Outs: religious practice, belief, perceptions of the Church and its ability to fulfill values, and parental characteristics. But we may not conclude that these empirical criteria are normative ones as well: although Ins believe and practice what they perceive to be the essentials of Catholicism, they still feel that their membership status is not contingent upon doing so. The borderline remains blurred in the sense that there is no universally accepted definition of what it takes to be Catholic. Thus it is still possible to find self-defined Catholics less overtly Catholic than others who have left the Church.

PART IV

Extensions

TEN

The Future of
These One Hundred

How likely is it that these people with whom I spoke in 1968 will change over time, and in what direction might they go? Does the deeper internalization of the desire to be a member of the Church on the part of most Ins mean they will not leave or rather that they will take longer to leave? If they remain members, will they become more or less orthodox? Will those Outs whose early history of Catholicism and interaction with their parents is similar to that of most Ins eventually return to the Church? Are they, indeed, merely on a sabbatical or a leave of absence?

One question that only time will answer is whether the position of the redefining In is a comfortable "halfway house" to being out, an extra step that he must take because the value of being Catholic is more central to him and harder to give up, or whether it is, in fact, as far as his exodus will go. Should he continue to consider himself a member of the Church, might his position be a "halfway house" across generations, a way of making it easier for his children to be Out? Many of these Ins are not strongly committed to the Catholic educational system (see Figure 6.4 and Table 6.6, Items 21 and 24) and may not enroll their children in Catholic schools. Without the support of formal Catholic education, will strong loyalties to the Church be produced in their children? Even though many of the present Ins are disenchanted with institutional Catholicism, it is not likely that they themselves could have been produced without it.

The possibility of Outs returning seems more remote than that of Ins leaving, despite the fact that fewer Outs exclude the possibility of a change of status. The border seems to be a point of no return with traffic going in one direction only: I found no Ins who said they had once left and later returned. If some Outs do return, however, the action may be prompted by their having children who reach school age, a point at which decisions Outs have made for themselves involve other people as well. Several of them already have had their children baptized. Should some of these Outs return, though, I cannot envisage that it will be to a formal Church resembling in many ways the one they left.

Some evidence bearing on the permanence of one's status comes from a follow-up questionnaire mailed to subjects who had been interviewed during the first half of the study. On July 29, 1969, almost four months after I began to interview, Pope Paul VI issued the encyclical *Humanae Vitae,* which reaffirmed traditional Catholic teaching banning the use of artificial contraception. In the middle of November, I mailed to the sixty-four subjects (40 Ins, 24 Outs) interviewed prior to that date a questionnaire that consisted of excerpts from quantified portions of the original one. The immediate purpose of this follow-up, although not revealed as such, was to see what effect the papal announcement had on the belief systems of Ins; but a secondary one was to indicate whether any people, Ins or Outs, had over the short space of four to seven months changed their status, beliefs, or perceptions of the Church.

How many of the questionnaires reached the subjects is unknown. Thirty of the forty Ins responded (75 per cent), and ten of the twenty-four Outs did (42 per cent). None of these subjects said they had changed their status, except for the female In mentioned in Chapter 8 and a male Out who previously had said he was "on leave" and now said he could not say whether he was in or out. The female In had been one of the exceptions to the association between Catholicism of the parent and current status of the offspring (Table 8.1).

Four to seven months is not a long period over which to test the permanence of a self-definition, and what permanence appears may be caused in part by the public commitment to a status taken by a subject at the time of the original interview. Yet what evidence we do have favors the conclusion that most of these 1968 definitions are fairly stable, as the subjects themselves predicted they would be.

The follow-up questionnaire also provides interesting data on its major point of attack, the belief systems of Ins (Table 10.1). Over the short period that intervened between the original interview and the follow-up, the thirty responding Ins showed a statistically significant decline in their average acceptance of the twenty beliefs, approaching closer to the zero point of the scale. The effect was contributed to equally by males and females.

On the key contraception item, Ins became more rejecting of what, in effect, was the pope's position. Males showed more of a change than females, but females continued to be the greater dissenters. Of all twenty beliefs, the one having the most significant drop was that on papal infallibility, Ins shifting from something less than "Possibly True" to something approaching "Possibly False." Thus the effect of the papal encyclical on these Ins was that of a boomerang: they moved in a direction opposite to that intended by the communicator, and the credibility of the communicator was diminished. The main effect was on subjects' understanding of the pope, not on their understanding of contraception.

The credibility of the institution the pope represents was also affected. A drop of about the same magnitude as on the

Table 10.1. Significant Differences in Thirty Responding Ins' Beliefs Before and After Papal Encyclical on Contraception

Belief No. and Type	50 Ins at Time of Interview	Before: 30 Ins at Time of Interview	After: 30 Ins on Mail Follow-up	Mean Before-After Difference	t	p < (2-tailed)
11 Church	.54	.67	− .60	1.27	4.41	.001
1 Church	.96	1.13	− .40	1.53	4.17	.001
15 Christ	2.32	2.40	1.77	.63	3.74	.001
5 Christ	2.58	2.63	1.93	.70	3.34	.01
20 Morality	−1.78	−1.70	−2.07	.37	2.26	.05
Average of 20 Items	.90	.97	.58	.39	3.03	.01

Note: Items are arranged in order of t values, which indicate the degree to which the distribution of the 30 Before scores is different from the distribution of the 30 After scores. For the full wording of each item, see Figure 4.1.

infallibility statement was seen in subjects' assent to "The Catholic Church is the one true Church." The move was from something stronger than "Possibly True" to something between "Possibly False" and "No Position."

Not as expected was the decline to a point below "Probably True" of the two statements interpretive of Christ, statements that had represented beliefs near the core of the In belief complex and ones that best distinguished Ins and Outs (Figure 4.1). Apparently the credibility of the figure who founded the institution and whom the pope is supposed to represent was affected by the encyclical. Contraception represented a "Man and This World" issue on which Ins had enough evidence of their own to take a position. They would not compromise on it, so that when consistency demanded the movement of some beliefs, the related "God and the Other World" doctrines were affected.

Such a reaction on the part of Ins means that the split between the institutional Church and their people's Church is a real one and one that is widening. The official representative of the institution did not have the power to move members in the direction he wished; he did not have the power to affect their In-Out status if they disagreed with him; nor, more remarkably, did he effect the slightest change in their perception of the thinking of the Church on contraception. Ins continued to think the Church was somewhere between "No Position" and "Possibly True" on what the pope said was "Definitely True." They did, however, see the Church as more monolithic and more a believer in an objective moral law after the encyclical.[1]

One implication of the results of the original interview and this follow-up is that theories of the "Protestant Ethic and the

---

1. See Figure 6.1 and Table 6.1, "Many Schools—One School"; follow-up mean was 2.50 ($t = 2.63$, $p < .02$, 2-tailed). See also Figure 6.2 and Table 6.4, Item 16; follow-up mean was 1.53 ($t = 2.73$, $p < .02$, 2-tailed). There were no other significant Before-After differences in the perception of the Church or of its beliefs.

Spirit of Capitalism" type are not applicable to these Catholics. Such theories explain the nonreligious behavior of a particular religious group by referring to the "official" ideological content of the religion in question and pointing to propositions there that justify, even cause, the behavior. Thus, Max Weber explained the historical rise of capitalism by focusing on the Protestant, and, in particular, the Calvinistic emphasis on ascetic performance of duty associated with one's station in life. Racial prejudice among church goers can be explained in similar fashion by pointing to the ethnocentric ("you are the chosen people") overtones of the religion in question. Or, to explain a conflict between religion and science, the part of a belief system that talks about man's ways of knowing ("faith over reason") is alluded to. In the socio-economic arena, religion is seen as the "opium of the people": statements of religion to the effect that the established political order is God's will prevent believers from becoming involved in social change. In all these instances, the part of the religion's belief system that interprets man and this world affects the overt behavior of the religion's adherents.

But on the subjects I interviewed such a dynamic has little hold. Their adherence to belief items about man and this world is not determined by the official ideology of their Catholic religion but by the same common evidence upon which non-Catholics base their judgment. Even though distinctive in other-worldly beliefs, they are not likely to be distinctive in beliefs affecting their overt behavior in society.

Orthodoxy in belief, like the borderline for Outs, appears to be a land of no return for these Ins. Over a relatively short period of time, they did show a decline in several significant areas. It is not likely that they will become more orthodox—nothing that the pope could say would affect them, and that pool of common evidence on which they rely will hardly move in the direction of orthodox Catholicism.

How readily these findings of a decline in orthodoxy may be generalized to American Catholics at large is difficult to say. Although the present subjects are representative of only some fraction of one per cent of American Catholics, they can be considered forerunners of what is to come. An increasing proportion of Catholics will be in the younger age brackets and attending college and graduate or professional school as the present subjects did and should undergo similar transitions in thought. Informal studies of two Catholic colleges show that these transitions are already happening in the area of belief.[2] We can also expect Catholicism to be more concerned with the products of its own educational system than with the forty-odd per cent who never heard of Vatican II, and so to move more in the direction of these subjects.

2. Surveys were taken by Rev. Bruce M. Ritter, O.F.M. Conv., at Manhattan College, New York (1967) and Rev. Robert Campbell, O.P., at DePaul University, Chicago (1963–1968).

ELEVEN

The Institution as Permeable: Past, Present, and Future

Let us now relax our attention on individuals, retreat some distance, and refocus on the total Church as an organization. Our concern will still be with the border, but now we will think of it as a membrane surrounding the entire Church. Our purpose will be to inquire about the permeability of that membrane, about its closedness or openness at various hierarchical levels to influence from the outside. We shall see how porous the border has been in the past, how porous it is now, and what we can expect of it in the future. We can then place our one hundred subjects in a context and at the same time speculate about the dynamics of the borderline.

Part of the job is for an historian, but since I am not that, we will have to make do with some simple diagrams of the Church over the past fifteen years. The Church can be depicted organizationally as a triangle, the apex representing the pope and the base all of the laity. In between the two are various levels of the hierarchy, bishops higher in rank than clergy and religious.

The perimeter of this triangle, which stands for the border of the organization, is drawn as a solid line to show that, in

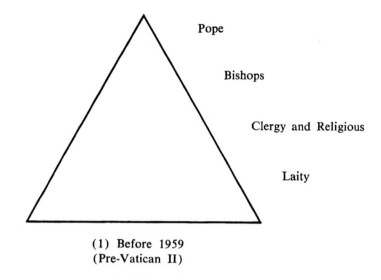

Pope

Bishops

Clergy and Religious

Laity

(1) Before 1959
(Pre-Vatican II)

the period before Vatican II, little influence from outside the Church was entering in. It is true that, prior to Pope John XXIII's announcement of an ecumenical council early in 1959, there were pockets of openness, renewals in embryo, within the Catholic Church: the Jesuit paleontologist Teilhard de Chardin was a well known individual example (Teilhard de Chardin, 1959); and even in America there was self-criticism within the Church regarding the lack of Catholic intellectuals (Ellis, 1955; O'Dea, 1958). While these pockets no doubt contributed to the spirit that led to the council, they were not numerous nor prominent within the American Church prior to 1959.

On January 25, 1959, Pope John announced that he would convoke the twenty-first ecumenical council to "let some fresh air into the Church." At this time talk of openness with other churches and liturgical change within the Catholic Church began to occur. Renewal and reform was anticipated, and with the convening of the council, we find that the border was more permeable at the upper levels of the hierarchy. There was expressed a desire to change and a new openness to the outside.

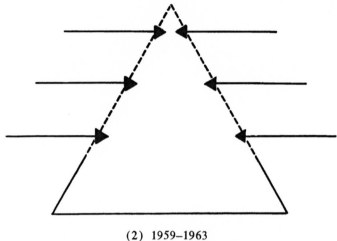

(2) 1959–1963
(Early Vatican II, including preparations)

As the council continued, enough time passed that the legitimacy of change and openness was conveyed downward through the hierarchy to members at lower levels of the Church. In late November of 1963, for example, the first draft of the declaration on religious freedom—hints of "civil rights legislation"—was presented at the council. This exposed for

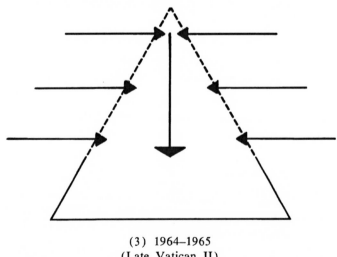

(3) 1964–1965
(Late Vatican II)

public debate the notion that one's own conscience is the ulti-mate criterion of belief and conduct. The legitimacy of open-ness and change, of thinking for oneself, traveled downward like a nerve impulse, and, like the impulse, it served to make porous the membrane surrounding the organization. Those dissatisfied with the Church yet dependent upon it both raised their hopes and expectations and were told they might be more independent. Others who might have left the Church were retained because no lines had been set as to the amount of change that might be forthcoming.

The council closed late in 1965 by formally passing the declaration on religious freedom, and the influence that it represented reached those of the laity who could be touched by it. Those who were near the border, by being in situations that kept them in contact with the world outside, responded with openness. At the same time, like the membrane at the trailing edge of the nerve impulse, the border around the upper hierarchy became impermeable to external forces. Paul VI, pope since 1963, sensed "immense, insidious dangers" within the Church and began to be hesitant in carrying on changes. A reactionary spirit, closing itself off from the outside, be-

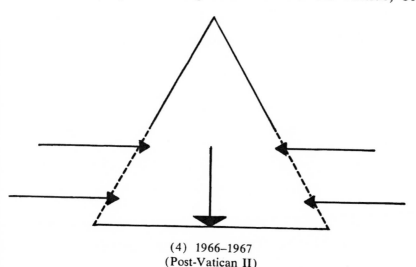

(4) 1966–1967
(Post-Vatican II)

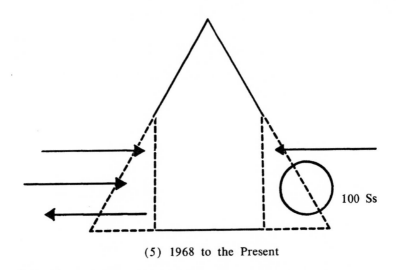

(5) 1968 to the Present

came characteristic of the upper hierarchy. Meanwhile, among the laity close to the border, the openings between inside and outside continued to dilate.

At the time I interviewed the one hundred subjects of this study (located on the periphery of the triangle), a number of things were occurring within the Church that affected the dynamics of the borderline. With his Credo of belief (June, 1968) and his encyclical on contraception (July, 1968), the pope at the apex became clearly and publicly conservative and closed to influence from the outside—as his reaction to dissension created by his encyclical confirms. Conservative Catholics at lower levels, those in the center who were never close to the border, began to resist the external influence flowing in, as they rejected some of the changes legitimated by the council. A line of defense began to form between them and the liberal-radicals. This silently developing schism created the outlines of the two Churches described in previous Chapters, the traditional Church of the hierarchy and the new Church of the people. Most of the upper hierarchy remains now in the center of the triangle, aligned with the traditional

Church, but a number of priests and even a few bishops position themselves on the side of the people's Church. An increasing proportion of these leave the priesthood. Some even abandon the Church.

Among the laity closest to the border, and these are especially young adults like those in the present study, there is movement outward from the Church: the number of exits increases. The ease with which I located Outs on two graduate campuses in 1968 (once I was plugged into the proper friendship circuits) makes me strongly suspect that leaving is on the upswing among this population—in 1962, only a small degree of apostasy among Catholics was found on graduate campuses of twelve top universities (Greeley, 1965). Since we have in-depth data on fifty of these Outs, let us take an intermission in our scenario and say something about the dynamics of legitimation and openness as they affect these individuals.

It is an oversimplification, I believe, to conceive of the major exodus pattern among these Outs as first a desire for freedom, then a leaving of the Catholic social and intellectual ghetto, a disenchantment with the Church, and an abandonment of it. One does not ordinarily become free of an institution he has depended on so long in such a straightforward manner. What appears to have happened is that upper levels of the organization first modified themselves, albeit slightly, and granted some independence to the members. They said in the general atmosphere that led to and surrounded Vatican II that people could think for themselves within the Church, that their individual conscience was the ultimate criterion of what they believed and how they acted, that the world outside must not be avoided but entered. It was the clergy—official representatives of the institution—who first raised the cry in the middle fifties: "Where are the Catholic intellectuals?" In other words, by some degree of change in the priests, theologians, and bishops who formally represented the Church, the upper levels sanctioned, legitimated, and in some cases encouraged those first steps that led members on a journey that would eventually carry some of them out of the Church.

The present subjects were tuned in to such institutional change. Forty-four Ins, for example, and forty Outs were aware of Vatican II's statement on freedom of conscience. During their transitions, seventeen of each group had been close to a priest or other religious figure who told them, in effect, "do your own thing" or even "I'm in the same boat you are." A number of them said that excellent courses in theology helped instigate the thought processes that led to their leaving. Nearly all were aware of officially Catholic models who had become extremely liberal or radical within the Church or who had left it.

That this increase of freedom in the institution led some to a conclusion the original "dispensers" of freedom would not have wished is not, in retrospect, surprising. The reactionary is quite right when he says that if some autonomy is granted by those in power, an increasing measure will be asked of them. Inches given lead to miles taken, we are told in the proverb. In 1965 Kenneth Clark predicted in print that "the closer the Negro community gets to the attainment of its goals . . . the more impatient will the Negro become for total equality." When led to think for themselves, young Catholics saw new horizons opened to them; their expectations rose. Though the layman began to enjoy a role in the Church he had not known for some time, he became aware that what he had was not enough. Having been given some measure of ideological freedom, he desired more. Not finding the new measure, and faced with the beginnings of a conservative reaction at the top of the organization (Vatican II became "Vacuum II" in the eyes of some), his frustration, ennui, or whatever increased to a point where he found himself one day outside the Church. To use the phrase of one subject, he "liberalized himself out."

If, indeed, more were abandoning the Church on graduate campuses in 1968 than in 1962, the timing of this exodus fits in nicely with the above postulation of a dynamic of initial legitimation by upper levels of the organization and subsequent rising expectation in those legitimated, with the expectations falling short of fulfillment. The year 1962 was one when "fresh air was being let into the Church," when the upper levels were publicly sanctioning some independent thought on the part of the members. Six years is an appropriate amount of time for such initial encouragement to snowball through rising expectations to a larger number of exits from the Church.

Such a dynamic was probably more characteristic of those Outs with stronger initial ties to the Church, that is, of those who had internalized the value of membership in a more profound way. Those with shallower internalization would probably have left the Church even had there been no sign of institutional change. Indeed, had there been no Vatican II, there could have been as many exits as we have found with Vatican II. The dynamics leading to exodus could have been otherwise, but, given the history of the sixties, it is likely that they were not.

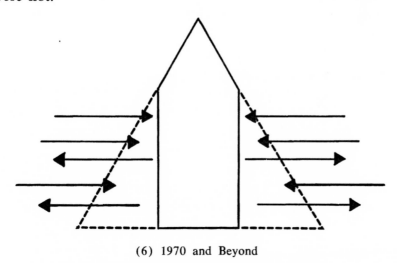

(6) 1970 and Beyond

As to the future, the Catholic Church appears headed in the direction of the diagram above. The border around the people's Church (which in reality are Churche*s*) is shown as more open than ever, so open in fact that the line between inside and outside is extremely blurred, less well defined than that between the two Churches. More, including some at upper levels, are leaving, but it is becoming difficult to speak of "leaving the Catholic Church," as if the Church were a single entity.[1] Out of that ill-defined mass (dotted lines), which was once an integral part of the organization, new forms of church life are beginning to emerge. Small clusters of people develop their own experimental communities or underground Churches. Some call themselves Catholic, some Christian, and others simply religious. Some are communities of believers and others include atheists and agnostics. Members of these cells are thus separatists within the total complex of Catholicism, but the separatism is diffuse and lacking definition. When there is a back door out of the organization, it can only be thus. For cohesion, definition, and force in a separatist movement, there must be no exit, a wall at the rear instead of a door.

Another characteristic of this Catholicism of the future is that the lines of resistance to outside influence—the hiatus between the two Churches—are now more clearly drawn, though no one speaks of schism because the Church is trying to heal 400 years of fractionation. These lines reach more deeply into the hierarchy, incorporating into the people's Church more of the upper clergy and bishops than before. Some of the hierarchy, then, is again open to the outside, but the majority remains entrenched in its closedness.

To understand this reaction, both the increased rigidity of the lines of resistance and the fact that this split extends farther up into the hierarchy, we have to realize that the state of the

1. As this book goes to press, I note that the *1970 Official Catholic Directory* (New York: P. J. Kennedy and Sons) reports the following decreased numerically from 1969: Catholic lay persons, priests, nuns, brothers, adult and infant baptisms, schools, students in Catholic schools, and places where Mass is celebrated. This is the first time since 1900 that the U.S. Catholic Church has declined in all these categories.

border described in the previous diagram is a threat to the organization. To see why this is so, and to understand how the Church appears to be responding to threat, we shall make some primitive comparisons of the Church with a nonvoluntary social system.

The Catholic Church is, after all, a voluntary social system; it is an organization that can be left. Indeed, only an act of the mind is necessary to cross the border. But a socio-economic order, for example, is not a voluntary social system. Someone at the bottom of the socio-economic ladder is not there voluntarily, nor can he easily leave his position if he wanted to. In one case, there is an out; in the other, there is not.

When change is desired but not forthcoming in a nonvoluntary social system, when the Outs of systems from which there is no out are backed up against a wall (yet impelled to extricate themselves from their condition), their only recourse appears to be an "ultimate act" against the system: taking to the streets, violence, anarchy. Such an act threatens the entire system.

A voluntary organization that does not change enough to meet the expectations of some, however, can be left, and the disenfranchised will not be backed up against a wall and turn to anarchy. All they will do is leave. But leaving is precisely what threatens the existence of the organization; it is the "ultimate act" against it, comparable to the violence that threatens the existence of the nonvoluntary social system. Both systems want to live; one dies by violent upheaval, the other by loss of members.

The ultimate acts, of course, are vastly different. One involves threat to the physical lives of members of the system. It is blatant and physically disruptive. The news media are always present to transmit the message of threat in hours, even minutes, throughout the entire system.

The threat caused by loss of members in a voluntary organization, however, is much less obvious, and in an organization like the Catholic Church in which there is little direct data to tell precisely how many are leaving, the threat is vague, slowly communicated, and much less a force for movement. But it is, nevertheless, like violence, a threat to the life of the system.

The responses of each kind of system to threat, whether by anarchy or abandonment, are similar. On the one hand, there is a response by some toward change, substantial change such as would not have occurred without the threat to life. Some of the major changes in religious communities and seminaries suffering from dropouts and a general lack of vocations (for which data is visible and unmistakable) suggest that threat to life is indeed producing change. In the Church of the future, we see that those near the border at upper levels, alarmed at what they perceive to be an exodus of important members, are attempting substantial change to prevent more from leaving and to incorporate some extremists within a new definition of the Church. Thus, as more clergy and bishops come into the people's Church, the border higher up becomes permeable once again. But as it does, a clearer line is formed between those higher up who are adapters and those who are not.

The above does not say that the violent in one case and the apostates in the other are the ones who actually go through the mechanics of effecting change. Anarchists do not riot to modify the existing system, nor do Outs leave to reform the Church. In the nonvoluntary system, the "liberals" at times perform the mechanics of change, their power enhanced because they are seen as able to save the system. In the voluntary Catholic Church, it is probably the redefining Ins, up and down the structure, whose power is also enhanced because they appear willing and able to remove the threat of a large number of exits and save the sinking ship.

For events at the border of the Catholic Church to so effect change, the institution, of course, must care about those who leave and perceive them as essential to the institution. Subjects like the present one hundred, the "cream of the crop" of Catholic education, must be disproportionately important to it, for they do represent only a tiny percent of American Catholics, and we cannot assume that American Catholics at large will leave as these fifty have.

If the response to threat of some who are high in the structure is change, the response of others is to control the threat and do nothing else. In the nonvoluntary system, we hear from these others the cry for law and order, a forcible control of those who would destroy the system. At the same time there is an attempt to curtail the efforts of those, high or low in the structure, who would use the fact of violent anarchy to try to effect change. These are seen as threatening because, while they do not seek to bring the system to ashes, they are after major, fundamental changes in it. That, to the controllers, is destroying the system by a different route.

In the Catholic Church, control by those in power can be exerted by expelling members, by drawing definitive lines around the Church to exclude those who would destroy the purity of the institution or compromise its traditional mission. Those who leave the institution, of course, do not need to be drummed out. But those who work for change, because of the threat they see in those who leave, are, in this sketch of the future, targets for the line-drawing controllers. They cannot be part of the Catholic Church, say the traditionalists, because they are threats to the purity of the institution. They, too, are seen as destroying the institution by a different route.

Thus, the line between the two Churches is made not only by those alienated from the institution but by those within who want to remove a threat. The line is more definitive and it extends higher up; but there is still great reluctance to speak of it publicly, and there is little desire on the part of the controllers to go through the formalities of excommunication. The Church is, after all, trying to heal an older split and does not want to take on a new one.

Just as we once saw a legitimating influence travelling downward through the organization and having the effect of opening up those near the border, so we have now a threatening influence travelling upward in the organization, which also has the effect of opening up those near the border. In each case the influence is resisted by those in the center of the triangle, and they form defenses against the forces entering the organization from the outside.

What is happening in the Catholic Church and what is yet to happen has been called by some a revolution. If we understand the ultimate act against the system in the parallel drawn above, there is some appropriateness to that term. A relatively small percentage of the people who occupy the system, legitimated by a few of those in power, have their expectations rise until they can no longer tolerate the system, and so they commit the ultimate act against it.

But to call recent events in the Catholic Church a revolution is to use, for the most part, an analogy. Where there is a door out, where the only thing required to break a stranglehold is a change of mind—a conversion, if you will—a large scale disruptive rebellion is not likely to occur. Only for those whose ties are strong, who set for themselves a wall at their backs, will the desire for change take on the compelling force of a revolution.

A Note on
Statistical Testing

The statistical procedures employed in this study (chiefly, analyses of variance yielding F scores, tests of mean differences yielding t scores, and χ^2 tests) are designed to indicate the probability that characteristics of a given sample reflect the characteristics of a population from which the sample is randomly drawn. Usually, the population is a specific finite one, e.g., all 1968 graduates of Catholic colleges in the United States. The p value associated with a particular F, t, or χ^2 score states what the chances are that the differences observed in the sample represent differences in the population at large. For example, if a sample male-female difference is significant with $p < .05$, we know that ninety-five times out of a hundred there will be at least some difference between males and females in the population from which the sample was drawn.

When research is not based on random sampling of a specific finite population, the population can be conceived of as the infinite number of measurements that could be taken of a phenomenon under exactly the same conditions that the present measurement is taken. In this case, the p value represents the probability that the present measurement reflects the value of the pool of this infinite population of measurements.

Clearly, the present investigation meets none of the requirements for which these inferential statistics are designed. The one hundred subjects were not randomly drawn from any specific population, nor could the conditions under which they were observed ever be replicated. What meaning, then, is attached to the F, t, and χ^2 scores, and what to the p values associated with them?

These statistics are used in this study—and, indeed, in much social psychological research—in a descriptive sense only. They indicate, better than simple mean differences or frequency counts, the extent to which one distribution of scores is different from another distribution of scores. The p value is given because it is a common denominator for F, t, and χ^2, and because it controls each statistic for the degrees of freedom involved in a particular comparison. In general, the practice of considering of importance only those differences significant at the $p < .05$ level has been followed here.

It should be noted that, as employed in this study, F, t, and χ^2 are descriptive of differences between the distributions of scores of two groups. F or t is used when the scores are on a ratio, interval, or ordinal scale, χ^2 when they are on a nominal scale. Differences, however, can also be thought of as associations: if Ins and Outs are distinguished on some characteristic, then being In is associated, for example, with a low value of the characteristic and being Out with a high value. There are statistics available that describe with coefficients of association what I have preferred to conceive of as differences (e.g., the contingent coefficient C, the point-biserial coefficient r_{pb}, the ϕ coefficient). The relation described by the coefficient is between two variables, one a two-point dichotomous variable (e.g., Ins and Outs) and the other the variable to which both groups respond (e.g., Belief Item 1). These coefficients of association can also be tested for their significance, i.e., for the probability that they reflect some association in the population at large.

My reasons for using statistics describing differences rather than statistics describing associations are that F, t, and χ^2 are more common vehicles of communication than are coefficients of association involving two-point dichotomous variables and that they fit better the major thrust of this study, which is precisely to search for differences, i.e., to establish some borderline between Ins and Outs that is not given in one's immediate perception of them.

The Questionnaire

SS#_____

Graduate School_____

Catholic College Attended_____

_____

Present Field of Study_____

_____

Source_____

_____

203

Time Started:_____

I. <u>Salience</u> <u>of</u> <u>Being</u> <u>Catholic</u>

1. At the present time, do you consider yourself a member of the
   Catholic Church?

   (1) Yes_____   (2) No_____

2. Do you wish to qualify your answer in any way?

   (1) Yes_____see below: (2) No_____

3. And being a Catholic has played a fairly important role in your life
   (at least at one time).

   (1) Yes_____   (2) No_____ (if no, terminate interview)

4-7. How important was it to you to be a Catholic at various times in
   your life? (Hand questionnaire to interviewee; have him check
   categories.)

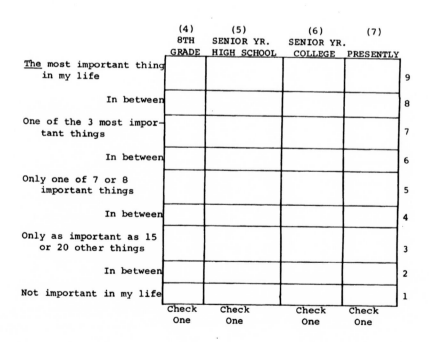

	(4) 8TH GRADE	(5) SENIOR YR. HIGH SCHOOL	(6) SENIOR YR. COLLEGE	(7) PRESENTLY	
The most important thing in my life					9
In between					8
One of the 3 most important things					7
In between					6
Only one of 7 or 8 important things					5
In between					4
Only as important as 15 or 20 other things					3
In between					2
Not important in my life					1
	Check One	Check One	Check One	Check One	

8-10. Did you attend: (8) a Catholic grammar school?
                             (1) Yes____   (2) No____
                        (9) a Catholic high school?
                             (1) Yes____   (2) No____
                       (10) a Catholic college?
                             (1) Yes____   (2) No____

11. Did you ever study to be a priest or religious?

                   (1) Yes____how long?_____
                   (2) No____

12. Was there a period in your life when you did not attend Mass
     regularly (90% of the time) on Sunday? (OUTS: before you left
     the Church)

                   (1) Yes____how long ago did the period begin?

                   how long did the period last?

                   (2) No____

13. Was there a period in your life when you attended Mass more than
     once a week?

                   (1) Yes____how long ago did the period begin?

                   how long did the period last?

                   how often did you attend (on the average)?

                   was attendance compulsory (e.g., at school)?

                   (2) No____

II. The Decision Process--(A) INS

Introduction: I have a set of different, but parallel, questions
for people with different experiences of member-
ship. Would you select the category below that
best describes the state of your membership in the
Church? (Have interviewee read the categories and
select the appropriate one.)

(1)_____I had left the Church for a period
of time and did not consider myself
a member.

--Now I clearly consider myself a
member.

(2)_____For a period of time I was half in
and half out of the Church, but I was
never definitely out.

--Now I clearly consider myself a
member.

(3)_____I have thought about leaving the
Church, but I never did leave, nor
was I even what you have called
"half in and half out."

--Now I clearly consider myself a
member.

(4)_____While I have never really thought
about leaving the Church as a possibility for myself, my reasons for
being a member have changed in the
past 10 years.

--Now I clearly consider myself a
member.

(5)_____My reasons for being a member of the
Church have not changed in the past
10 years.

--Now I clearly consider myself a
member.

IN categories #1, 2, 3 begin here:

1. How long have you been a member of the Church?

2. When did you first begin to think about leaving the Church?

   (Get definite point in time):

3. When would you say it was clear to you that you still wished to be a member of the Church?

   (Get definite point in time):

4. Therefore, from the time you first began to think about leaving until the time it was clear to you that you still wished to be a member was about...

   _____
                        (time)

5. How much of a crisis was involved in all this? By "crisis" I mean the feeling of indecision, anxiety, pressure, and so on.

6. Let me read you some categories describing amount of crisis. Pick the one that best fits your situation with regard to the Church.

   (9)_____The biggest crisis in my life
   (8)_____In between
   (7)_____One of the three biggest crises
   (6)_____In between
   (5)_____Only one of the 7 or 8 biggest crises
   (4)_____In between
   (3)_____Only as big as 15 or 20 other crises
   (2)_____In between
   (1)_____Not a crisis in my life

7. At any point in this process did you come to a _decision_ to remain in the Church?

   (1) Yes_____
   (2) No_____
   (3) Other_____record verbatim:

8. Was there any concrete situation or incident that accompanied your decision (if there was one)?

        (1)   Yes_____describe briefly:

        (2)   No_____

9. Was there any concrete act by which you reconfirmed or reinstated membership--something you did or stopped doing?

        (1)   Yes_____describe briefly:

        (2)   No_____

10. What were your reasons for remaining in the Church?
(After listing them, read them back to interviewee and have him rank them in order of importance.)

11. Were there any incidents, experiences, or situations of <u>yours</u> (long or short term) that made you wish to remain in the Church?

12. Was there anything anyone <u>connected</u> <u>with</u> <u>the</u> <u>Church</u> did or did
    not do (long or short term) to make you wish to remain in the
    Church?

13. Would you have left just to get away from the Church (1)_____
    or were you actively turning to something else (5)_____?

                                        (2) getting away_____
    In between (do not suggest), but closer to (3) neither_____
                                        (4) turning to_____

14. Could you describe what you would have changed <u>to</u>?
    (If nothing in particular, enter "nothing.")

15. Does this mean or include: (Read categories. Check most appropri-
                                  ate item.)

        (1)_____no religion, atheist
        (2)_____no religion, though not atheist
        (3)_____a personal religion, with no affiliation with
                      any religious group
        (4)_____a broad Catholicism
        (5)_____a broad Christianity
        (6)_____a particular Protestant religion:_____
        (7)_____a particular non-Christian religion:_____

16. What did it feel like being in the Church after you started thinking
    of leaving--but before you decided to remain?

17. What does it feel like being in the Church now?

IN category #4 begin here:

1. How long have you been a member of the Church?

2. Can you point to a time when your reasons for being a member began to change?

        (1) Yes_____
        (2) No_____

3. IF YES: When did your reasons begin to change?

(Get definite point in time):

4. Are your reasons for being a member of the Church pretty well settled now (1)_____, or are you still in the process of changing them (5)_____?

                                      (2) settled_____
In between (do not suggest), but closer to (3) neither_____
                                      (4) changing_____

5. IF SETTLED (OR CLOSER TO SETTLED): About when were they settled?

(Get definite point in time):

        Therefore, from the time your reasons began to change until they became pretty well settled was about...

                _____
                                   (time)

6. How much of a crisis was involved in all this? By "crisis" I mean the feeling of indecision, anxiety, pressure, and so on.

7. Let me read you some categories describing amount of crisis. Pick the one that best fits your situation with regard to the Church.

        (9)_____The biggest crisis in my life
        (8)_____In between
        (7)_____One of the three biggest crises
        (6)_____In between
        (5)_____Only one of the 7 or 8 biggest crises
        (4)_____In between
        (3)_____Only as big as 15 or 20 other crises
        (2)_____In between
        (1)_____Not a crisis in my life

8. Before they changed, what were your reasons for being a member of
    the Church?   (After listing them, read them back to interviewee
    and have him rank them in order of importance.)

9. After they changed, what were your reasons for being a member of
    the Church?   (After listing them, read them back to interviewee
    and have him rank them in order of importance.)

IN category #5 begin here:

1. How long have you been a member of the Church?

2. Ten years ago, what were your reasons for being a member of the Church? (After listing them, read them back to interviewee and have him rank them in order of importance.)

3. Five years ago, what were your reasons for being a member of the Church? (After listing them, read them back to interviewee and have him rank them in order of importance.)

4. What are your reasons for being a member of the Church now? (After listing them, read them back to interviewee and have him rank them in order of importance.)

18. Do (did) you have any close contact with a priest or religious?

> (2) No_____
> (1) Yes_____(Include relationships that merely border
>   on closeness.)
>
> > No. of contacts_____
> > Priest_____Nun_____Brother_____Scholastic_____
> > Other (specify)_____
> >
> > Relationship of principle contact to you
> > around time of X (whatever X was: leaving
> > and returning, half-out, thinking about
> > leaving, changing reasons, maintaining
> > reasons):
> >
> >
> > Did you know him (her) before_____after_____
> > both_____your X?
> >
> > Did he (she) know about your X? Yes_____
> >   No_____
> >   Don't know___
> >
> > What was his (her) reaction?

19. How many Catholic magazines, periodicals, or newspapers do (did)
     you read regularly?

> (a) before X_____principle one:_____
>
> (b) after X_____principle one:_____

20. How many books having something to do with Catholicism have you
     read:

> (a) in the year before X:_____best one:_____
>
> (b) in the past year, or since X:_____
>   best one:_____

21. Are you aware of Vatican II's statement on freedom of conscience?

> (2) No_____
> (1) Yes_____
>
> > Did you become aware of it before_____or
> > after_____X? At the same time_____?
> >
> > What was your reaction to it?

22. Since X, do you maintain contact with more (1)_____, fewer (3)_____, or about the same number (2)_____of non-Catholic friends?

23. Since X, do you maintain contact with more (1)_____, fewer (3)_____, or about the same number (2)_____of Catholic friends?

24. How many good friends of yours have left the Church?_____

25. How many good friends of yours have gone through roughly the same process that you have (and are still in the Church)?_____

26. Are there any teachings or doctrines of the Church that you find especially unattractive or false? (Indicate briefly. Rank.)

27. Is there anything else about the Church that you especially dislike, or find not admirable? (Indicate briefly. Rank.)

28. Then why are you still a member of the Church? I ask this not to challenge you, but to help me clarify your thoughts by setting up a contrast to them.

29. What do you feel you gain by being a member?

30. What do you feel you lose by be. ıg a member?

31. Do you think you will ever change your present philosophy of life?

        (1)   Yes_____

        (2)   No_____

        (3)   Other_____record verbatim:

32. IF ANYTHING BUT NO: Do you have any idea what the change might be?

        Do you have any idea when it might come?

33. Do you think you will ever give up Catholicism?

        (1)   Yes_____

        (2)   No_____

        (3)   Other_____record verbatim:

34. IF YES: Under what circumstances?

        When might this be?

35. IF NO: Under no circumstances whatever?
           (Get circumstances if listed.)

II. The Decision Process--(B) OUTS

1. How long had you been a member of the Church?

2. When did you first begin to think about leaving the Church?

(Get definite point in time):

3. When would you say it was clear to you that you no longer wished to be a member of the Church?

(Get definite point in time):

4. Therefore, from the time you first began to think about leaving until the time it was clear to you that you no longer wished to be a member was about...

(time)

5. How much of a crisis was involved in all this? By "crisis" I mean the feeling of indecision, anxiety, pressure, and so on.

6. Let me read you some categories describing amount of crisis. Pick the one that best fits your situation with regard to the Church.

(9)_____The biggest crisis in my life
(8)_____In between
(7)_____One of the three biggest crises
(6)_____In between
(5)_____Only one of the 7 or 8 biggest crises
(4)_____In between
(3)_____Only as big as 15 or 20 other crises
(2)_____In between
(1)_____Not a crisis in my life

7. At any point in this process did you come to a decision to leave the Church?

(1) Yes_____
(2) No_____
(3) Other_____record verbatim:

8. Was there any concrete situation or incident that accompanied your decision (if there was one)?

        (1) Yes_____describe briefly:

        (2) No_____

9. Was there any concrete act by which you gave up membership--something you did or stopped doing?

        (1) Yes_____describe briefly:

        (2) No_____

10. What were your reasons for leaving the Church?
    (After listing them, read them back to interviewee and have him rank them in order of importance.)

11. Were there any incidents, experiences, or situations of <u>yours</u> (long or short term) that made you wish to leave the Church?

12. Was there anything that anyone connected with the Church did or did not do (long or short term) to make you wish to leave the Church?

13. Was your leaving a matter of just getting away from the Church (1)_____, or were you actively turning to something else (5)_____?

    In between (do not suggest), but closer to   (2) getting away_____
      (3) neither_____
      (4) turning to_____

14. Could you describe what you have changed to?
    (If nothing in particular, enter "nothing.")

15. Does this mean or include: (Read categories. Check most appropriate item.)

    (1)_____no religion, atheist
    (2)_____no religion, though not atheist
    (3)_____a personal religion, with no affiliation with any religious group
    (4)_____a broad Catholicism
    (5)_____a broad Christianity
    (6)_____a particular Protestant religion:_____
    (7)_____a particular non-Christian religion:_____

16. What did it feel like being in the Church after you started thinking of leaving--but before you left?

17. What did (and does) it feel like being out of the Church?

18. Before leaving, did you have any close contact with a priest or religious?

        (2) No_____
        (1) Yes_____(Include relationships that merely border
                    on closeness.)

                No. of contacts_____
                Priest_____Nun_____Brother_____Scholastic_____
                Other (specify)_____

                Relationship of principle contact to you:

                Did he (she) know about your leaving the
                Church?
                      Yes_____
                      No_____
                      Don't know_____

                What was his (her) reaction?

19. Do you now have any close contact with a priest or religious?

        (2) No_____
        (1) Yes_____

                No. of contacts_____Same ones as before?_____
                Priest_____Nun_____Brother_____Scholastic_____
                Other (specify)_____

                Relationship of principle contact to you:

                Does he (she) know that you are out of the
                Church?
                      Yes_____
                      No_____
                      Don't know_____

                What is his (her) reaction to it?

20. How many Catholic magazines, periodicals, or newspapers do (did) you read regularly?

        (a) before you left:_____principle one:_____

        (b) after you left:_____principle one:_____

21. How many books having something to do with Catholicism have you read:

        (a) in the year before you left:_____best one:_____

        (b) in the past year, or since you left:_____

                best one:_____

22. Are you aware of Vatican II's statement on freedom of conscience?

      (2) No_____
      (1) Yes_____

               Did you become aware of it before_____ or
               after_____you left? At the same time_____.

               What was your reaction to it?

23. Since leaving the Church, do you maintain contact with more (1)_____, fewer (3)_____, or about the same number (2)_____ of non-Catholic friends?

24. Since leaving the Church, do you maintain contact with more (1)_____, fewer (3)_____, or about the same number (2)_____ of Catholic friends?

25. How many good friends of yours have also left the Church?

26. Are there any teaching or doctrines of the Church that you find especially attractive or true? (Indicate briefly. Rank.)

27. Is there anything else about the Church that you especially like or admire? (Indicate briefly. Rank.)

28. They why did you leave the Church? I ask this not to challenge you, but to help me clarify your thoughts by setting up a contrast to them.

29. What do you feel you have gained by leaving?

30. What do you feel you have lost by leaving?

31. Do you think you will ever change your present philosophy of life?

        (1) Yes_____
        (2) No_____
        (3) Other_____record verbatim:

32. IF ANYTHING BUT NO: Do you have any idea what the change might be?

        Do you have any idea of when it might come?

33. Do you think you will ever change back to Catholicism?

        (1) Yes_____
        (2) No_____
        (3) Other_____record verbatim:

34. IF YES: Under what circumstances?

        When might this be?

35. IF NO: Under no circumstances whatever?
            (Get circumstances if listed.)

III. Values

> Introduction: In order to fit the preceding into some sort of
> context, I would like to ask you some questions
> about the things you value in life, and then ask
> you how membership in the Church affects (affected)
> the attainment of those values.

1. What two things would you most like to accomplish in life?
(After listing them, have interviewee rank them in order of importance.)

2. What two people (living or dead) do you admire the most? What do
you admire about each? (After listing them, have interviewee rank
them in order of importance.)

3. What is the major lesson you have learned from life?

4. What cause would you most like to see succeed?

5. What cause would you most like to see fail?

6. Does (would) being a member of the Church hinder or help you in
    accomplishing what you want to accomplish? (Read categories.)

    Goal ranked first: (1) Hinders_____   (2) Slightly Hinders_____

                         (3) Neither Hinders nor Helps_____

                         (4) Slightly Helps_____   (5) Helps_____

    Goal ranked second: (1) Hinders_____   (2) Slightly Hinders_____

                         (3) Neither Hinders nor Helps_____

                         (4) Slightly Helps_____   (5) Helps_____

7. What is (was) the attitude of the people you admire the most
    toward the Church? (Read categories.)

    Person ranked first: (1) Negative_____   (2) Slightly Negative_____

                           (3) Neutral_____

                           (4) Slightly Positive_____   Positive_____

    Person ranked second: (1) Negative_____   (2) Slightly Negative_____

                           (3) Neutral_____

                           (4) Slightly Positive_____   (5) Positive_____

8. Is the Church involved positively or negatively in the major lesson you have learned from life? (Read categories. Note that the answer yields <u>resultant</u> attitude toward the Church.)

   (1) Negatively_____ (2) Slightly Negative_____

   (3) Neutral_____

   (4) Slightly Positive_____ (5) Positively_____

9. Is the Church hindering or helping the cause you would most like to see succeed? Or is the Church irrelevant to it? (Read categories.)

   (1) Hindering_____ (2) Slightly Hindering_____

   (3) Irrelevant_____

   (4) Slightly Helping_____ (5) Helping_____

10. Is the Church hindering or helping the cause you would most like to see fail? Or is the Church irrelevant to it? (Read categories.)

   (1) Hindering_____ (2) Slightly Hindering_____

   (3) Irrelevant_____

   (4) Slightly Helping_____ (5) Helping_____

Values Quantified--Instructions:

The purpose of the next part of the questionnaire is to get some of
the preceding into quantified form.

The sheets that follow contain a list of values that people have and
also a scale on which you can rate how important these values are in
your life. The idea is to indicate how much satisfaction these values
give you now or would give you if you achieved them.

Note the wording of the scale. Because some of these values overlap,
you may end up circling as many as 4 or 5 items under the heading
"One of the 3 most important things." On the other hand, you may end
up circling only 1 or 2.

I would suggest reading through the list once again to get an idea of
what is there, and then going back and asking yourself for each individual item, "How important is this in my life?" We are looking for
what you really value, not what you feel you ought to value.

	Not important in my life	In Between	Only as important as 15 or 20 other things	In Between	Only one of 7 or 8 important things	In Between	One of the 3 most important things	In Between	The most important thing in my life
1. Living for God alone.	0	1	2	3	4	5	6	7	8
2. Having personal, meaningful ties with other human beings.	0	1	2	3	4	5	6	7	8
3. Being happily married and having a family.	0	1	2	3	4	5	6	7	8
4. Having a stable philosophy of life.	0	1	2	3	4	5	6	7	8
5. Having my beliefs, values, and assumptions shaken up	0	1	2	3	4	5	6	7	8
6. Making a significant contribution in the intellectual community.	0	1	2	3	4	5	6	7	8
7. Having dependable people in authority to rely on.	0	1	2	3	4	5	6	7	8
8. Being able to think and act for myself.	0	1	2	3	4	5	6	7	8

	Not important in my life	In Between	Only as important as 15 or 20 other things	In Between	Only one of 7 or 8 important things	In Between	One of the 3 most important things	In Between	The most important thing in my life
9. Having interesting and worthwhile work to do.	0	1	2	3	4	5	6	7	8
10. Becoming a full human being.	0	1	2	3	4	5	6	7	8
11. Spreading the message of Christ.	0	1	2	3	4	5	6	7	8
12. Accomplishing something for the underprivileged, the poverty-stricken.	0	1	2	3	4	5	6	7	8
13. Escaping the confines of my early background.	0	1	2	3	4	5	6	7	8
14. Remaining loyal to the truths I was taught growing up.	0	1	2	3	4	5	6	7	8
15. Having a satisfactory sexual outlet.	0	1	2	3	4	5	6	7	8
16. Being able to determine my own code of morality.	0	1	2	3	4	5	6	7	8

	Not important in my life	In Between	Only as important as 15 or 20 other things	In Between	Only one of 7 or 8 important things	In Between	One of the 3 most important things	In Between	The most important thing in my life
17. Following the precepts of God in my moral actions.	0	1	2	3	4	5	6	7	8
18. Accomplishing something for the cause of world peace.	0	1	2	3	4	5	6	7	8
19. Atoning for my sins.	0	1	2	3	4	5	6	7	8
20. Being able to live with some of my inadequacies.	0	1	2	3	4	5	6	7	8
21. OUTS ONLY: Being _____ (whatever you are)	0	1	2	3	4	5	6	7	8
22. INS ONLY: Being a Catholic.	0	1	2	3	4	5	6	7	8

Instrumentality of Membership

Instructions: This section of the questionnaire involves rating how membership in the Catholic Church is related to the attainment of your values. The list of values will be presented again, and you are to indicate whether--in your situation--being a member of the Catholic Church hinders (or would hinder), helps (or would help) the attainment of each value. You may also see membership as neutral to the attainment of the value.

I would suggest you forget about whether or not the values were important to you, and concentrate only on whether being a member of the Church helps in attaining the value.

	(would) HINDERS	(would) SLIGHTLY HINDERS	(would) NEITHER helps nor hinders	(would) SLIGHTLY HELPS	(would) HELPS	
Being a member of the Catholic Church...	-2	-1	0	+1	+2	...living for God alone. (1)
"	-2	-1	0	+1	+2	...having personal, meaningful ties with other human beings. (2)
"	-2	-1	.0	+1	+2	...being happily married and having a family. (3)
"	-2	-1	0	+1	+2	...having a stable philosophy of life. (4)
"	-2	-1	0	+1	+2	...having my beliefs, values, and assumptions shaken up from time to time. (5)

Being a member of the Catholic Church...	(would) HINDERS	(would) SLIGHTLY HINDERS	(would) NEITHER helps nor hinders	(would) SLIGHTLY HELPS	(would) HELPS	
	-2	-1	0	+1	+2	...making a significant contri- (6) bution in the intellectual community
"	-2	-1	0	+1	+2	...having dependable people in (7) authority to rely on.
"	-2	-1	0	+1	+2	...being able to think and act (8) for myself.
"	-2	-1	0	+1	+2	...having interesting and worth-(9) while work to do.
"	-2	-1	0	+1	+2	...becoming a full human being.(10)
"	-2	-1	0	+1	+2	...spreading the message of (11) Christ.
"	-2	-1	0	+1	+2	...accomplishing something for (12) the underprivileged, the poverty-stricken.
"	-2	-1	0	+1	+2	...escaping the confines of my (13) early background.

Being a member of the Catholic Church...	(would) HINDERS	(would) SLIGHTLY HINDERS	(would) NEITHER helps nor hinders	(would) SLIGHTLY HELPS	(would) HELPS	
"	-2	-1	0	+1	+2	...remaining loyal to the truths I was taught growing up. (14)
"	-2	-1	0	+1	+2	...having a satisfactory sexual outlet. (15)
"	-2	-1	0	+1	+2	...being able to determine my own code of morality. (16)
"	-2	-1	0	+1	+2	...following the precepts of God in my moral actions. (17)
"	-2	-1	0	+1	+2	...accomplishing something for the cause of world peace. (18)
"	-2	-1	0	+1	+2	...atoning for my sins. (19)
"	-2	-1	0	+1	+2	...being able to live with some of my inadequacies. (20)

IV. Inventory of Beliefs: (A) Self

Instructions: On these sheets are contained a list of statements. Indicate whether you believe these statements, as they stand, are true or false. Also indicate your degree of certitude in saying something is true or false: you may feel that a statement is (1) possible, (2) probably, or (3) definitely true or false. It may also be the case that you have no position on the matter one way or the other (0).

	Definitely FALSE	Probably FALSE	Possibly FALSE	No position one way or the other	Possibly TRUE	Probably TRUE	Definitely TRUE
1. The Catholic Church is the one true Church.	-3	-2	-1	0	+1	+2	+3
2. Mortification of the flesh is essential to human perfection.	-3	-2	-1	0	+1	+2	+3
3. There is a God.	-3	-2	-1	0	+1	+2	+3
4. Premarital sexual intercourse is morally wrong.	-3	-2	-1	0	+1	+2	+3
5. Christ rose from the dead.	-3	-2	-1	0	+1	+2	+3
6. Every man has an immortal, spiritual soul.	-3	-2	-1	0	+1	+2	+3
7. In conceiving and giving birth to Our Lord, Mary retained her virginity.	-3	-2	-1	0	+1	+2	+3

	Definitely FALSE	Probably FALSE	Possibly FALSE	No position one way or the other	Possibly TRUE	Probably TRUE	Definitely TRUE
8. Deliberately missing Mass on Sunday is a mortal sin.	-3	-2	-1	0	+1	+2	+3
9. There is a state of eternal reward called heaven.	-3	-2	-1	0	+1	+2	+3
10. Man has a free will and is responsible for his action, both good and evil.	-3	-2	-1	0	+1	+2	+3
11. The pope is infallible when speaking on matters of faith and morals.	-3	-2	-1	0	+1	+2	+3
12. Abortion is morally wrong.	-3	-2	-1	0	+1	+2	+3
13. There are three Persons in one God.	-3	-2	-1	0	+1	+2	+3
14. People can be divided into two distinct classes: those in the state of grace and those not in the state of grace.	-3	-2	-1	0	+1	+2	+3
15. Christ is really present in the Eucharist.	-3	-2	-1	0	+1	+2	+3
16. There is an objective moral law valid for all men of all times.	-3	-2	-1	0	+1	+2	+3

	Definitely FALSE	Probably FALSE	Possibly FALSE	No position one way or the other	Possibly TRUE	Probably TRUE	Definitely TRUE
17. Mary's body was assumed into heaven.	-3	-2	-1	0	+1	+2	+3
18. Every man is born with original sin.	-3	-2	-1	0	+1	+2	+3
19. There is a state of eternal punishment called hell.	-3	-2	-1	0	+1	+2	+3
20. The use of artificial contraceptives is morally wrong.	-3	-2	-1	0	+1	+2	+3
21. The parochial school system should be allowed to phase out of existence.	-3	-2	-1	0	+1	+2	+3
22. Priests should retain their obligation of celibacy.	-3	-2	-1	0	+1	+2	+3
23. The Catholic Church should show less caution in pursuing the ecumenical movement.	-3	-2	-1	0	+1	+2	+3
24. The boards of trustees of Catholic universities should remain in the hands of priests and/or religious.	-3	-2	-1	0	+1	+2	+3
25. The Catholic Church should continue her mission to bring all people into her fold.	-3	-2	-1	0	+1	+2	+3

	Definitely FALSE	Probably FALSE	Possibly FALSE	No position one way or the other	Possibly TRUE	Probably TRUE	Definitely TRUE
26. Nuns should be free to adopt contemporary dress.	-3	-2	-1	0	+1	+2	+3
27. Planned parenthood clinics should be set up in depressed areas of the United States and the world.	-3	-2	-1	0	+1	+2	+3
28. The United States should stand firm in its present position on Vietnam.	-3	-2	-1	0	+1	+2	+3
29. Negro students should be bused to all-white schools to promote racial integration.	-3	-2	-1	0	+1	+2	+3
30. The Catholic belief system as a whole is ...	-3	-2	-1	0	+1	+2	+3
31. When being a Catholic was most important to me, the Catholic belief system as a whole appeared...	-1	-2	-1	0	+1	+2	+3

(B) Church

Instructions: Now would you go through these statements a second time and indicate what you believe is the thinking of the Church--as you define the Church--on these matters? Also, as above, indicate the degree of certitude that you believe that the Church has.

	Definitely FALSE	Probably FALSE	Possibly FALSE	No position one way or the other	Possibly TRUE	Probably TRUE	Definitely TRUE
1. The Catholic Church is the one true Church.	-3	-2	-1	0	+1	+2	+3
2. Mortification of the flesh is essential to human perfection.	-3	-2	-1	0	+1	+2	+3
3. There is a God.	-3	-2	-1	0	+1	+2	+3
4. Premarital sexual intercourse is morally wrong.	-3	-2	-1	0	+1	+2	+3
5. Christ rose from the dead.	-3	-2	-1	0	+1	+2	+3
6. Every man has an immortal, spiritual soul.	-3	-2	-1	0	+1	+2	+3
7. In conceiving and giving birth to Our Lord, Mary retained her virginity.	-3	-2	-1	0	+1	+2	+3

	Definitely FALSE	Probably FALSE	Possibly FALSE	No position one way or the other	Possibly TRUE	Probably TRUE	Definitely TRUE
8. Deliberately missing Mass on Sunday is a mortal sin.	-3	-2	-1	0	+1	+2	+3
9. There is a state of eternal reward called heaven.	-3	-2	-1	0	+1	+2	+3
10. Man has a free will and is responsible for his actions, both good and evil.	-3	-2	-1	0	+1	+2	+3
11. The pope is infallible when speaking on matters of faith and morals.	-3	-2	-1	0	+1	+2	+3
12. Abortion is morally wrong.	-3	-2	-1	0	+1	+2	+3
13. There are three Persons in one God.	-3	-2	-1	0	+1	+2	+3
14. People can be divided into two distinct classes: those in the state of grace and those not in the state of grace.	-3	-2	-1	0	+1	+2	+3
15. Christ is really present in the Eucharist.	-3	-2	-1	0	+1	+2	+3
16. There is an objective moral law valid for all men o⁻ all times.	-3	-2	-1	0	+1	+2	+3

	Definitely FALSE	Probably FALSE	Possibly FALSE	No position one way or the other	Possibly TRUE	Probably TRUE	Definitely TRUE
17. Mary's body was assumed into heaven.	-3	-2	-1	0	+1	+2	+3
18. Every man is born with original sin.	-3	-2	-1	0	+1	+2	+3
19. There is a state of eternal punishment called hell.	-3	-2	-1	0	+1	+2	+3
20. The use of artificial contraceptives is morally wrong.	-3	-2	-1	0	+1	+2	+3
21. The parochial school system should be allowed to phase out of existence.	-3	-2	-1	0	+1	+2	+3
22. Priests should retain their obligation of celibacy.	-3	-2	-1	0	+1	+2	+3
23. The Catholic Church should show less caution in pursuing the ecumenical movement.	-3	-2	-1	0	+1	+2	+3
24. The boards of trustees of Catholic universities should remain in the hands of priests and/or religious.	-3	-2	-1	0	+1	+2	+3
25. The Catholic Church should continue her mission to bring all people into her fold.	-3	-2	-1	0	+1	+2	+3

	Definitely FALSE	Probably FALSE	Possibly FALSE	No position one way or the other	Possibly TRUE	Probably TRUE	Definitely TRUE
26. Nuns should be free to adopt contemporary dress.	-3	-2	-1	0	+1	+2	+3
27. Planned parenthood clinics should be set up in depressed areas of the United States and the world.	-3	-2	-1	0	+1	+2	+3
28. The United States should stand firm in its present position on Vietnam.	-3	-2	-1	0	+1	+2	+3
29. Negro students should be bused to all-white schools to promote racial integration.	-3	-2	-1	0	+1	+2	+3
30. The Catholic belief system as a whole is...	-3	-2	-1	0	+1	+2	+3

(C) Parents

Instructions: Now go through these statements a final time and indicate what you believe is the thinking of your parents on these matters. Also, as above, indicate the degree of certitude that you believe your parents have.

(If only one parent practices Catholicism, indicate his/her thought. If both practice, indicate what would be their combined thought.)

Please fill in: The following represents the thought of mother _____, father _____, both _____.

	Definitely FALSE	Probably FALSE	Possibly FALSE	No position one way or the other	Possibly TRUE	Probably TRUE	Definitely TRUE
1. The Catholic Church is the one true Church.	-3	-2	-1	0	+1	+2	+3
2. Mortification of the flesh is essential to human perfection.	-3	-2	-1	0	+1	+2	+3
3. There is a God.	-3	-2	-1	0	+1	+2	+3
4. Premarital sexual intercourse is morally wrong.	-3	-2	-1	0	+1	+2	+3
5. Christ rose from the dead.	-3	-2	-1	0	+1	+2	+3
6. Every man has an immortal, spiritual soul.	-3	-2	-1	0	+1	+2	+3
7. In conceiving and giving birth to Our Lord, Mary retained her virginity.	-3	-2	-1	0	+1	+2	+3

	Definitely FALSE	Probably FALSE	Possibly FALSE	No position one way or the other	Possibly TRUE	Probably TRUE	Definitely TRUE
8. Deliberately missing Mass on Sunday is a mortal sin.	-3	-2	-1	0	+1	+2	+3
9. There is a state of eternal reward called heaven.	-3	-2	-1	0	+1	+2	+3
10. Man has a free will and is responsible for his actions, both good and evil.	-3	-2	-1	0	+1	+2	+3
11. The pope is infallible when speaking on matters of faith and morals.	-3	-2	-1	0	+1	+2	+3
12. Abortion is morally wrong.	-3	-2	-1	0	+1	+2	+3
13. There are three Persons in one God.	-3	-2	-1	0	+1	+2	+3
14. People can be divided into two distinct classes: those in the state of grace and those not in the state of grace.	-3	-2	-1	0	+1	+2	+3
15. Christ is really present in the Eucharist.	-3	-2	-1	0	+1	+2	+3
16. There is an objective moral law valid for all men of all times.	-3	-2	-1	0	+1	+2	+3

	Definitely FALSE	Probably FALSE	Possibly FALSE	No position one way or the other	Possibly TRUE	Probably TRUE	Definitely TRUE
17. Mary's body was assumed into heaven.	-3	-2	-1	0	+1	+2	+3
18. Every man is born with original sin.	-3	-2	-1	0	+1	+2	+3
19. There is a state of eternal punishment called hell.	-3	-2	-1	0	+1	+2	+3
20. The use of artificial contraceptives is morally wrong.	-3	-2	-1	0	+1	+2	+3
21. The parochial school system should be allowed to phase out of existence.	-3	-2	-1	0	+1	+2	+3
22. Priests should retain their obligation of celibacy.	-3	-2	-1	0	+1	+2	+3
23. The Catholic Church should show less caution in pursuing the ecumenical movement.	-3	-2	-1	0	+1	+2	+3
24. The boards of trustees of Catholic universities should remain in the hands of priests and/or religious.	-3	-2	-1	0	+1	+2	+3
25. The Catholic Church should continue her mission to bring all people into her fold.	-3	-2	-1	0	+1	+2	+3

	Definitely FALSE	Probably FALSE	Possibly FALSE	No position one way or the other	Possibly TRUE	Probably TRUE	Definitely TRUE
26. Nuns should be free to adopt contemporary dress.	-3	-2	-1	0	+1	+2	+3
27. Planned parenthood clinics should be set up in depressed areas of the United States and world.	-3	-2	-1	0	+1	+2	+3
28. The United States should stand firm in its present position on Vietnam.	-3	-2	-1	0	+1	+2	+3
29. Negro students should be bused to all-white schools to promote racial integration.	-3	-2	-1	0	+1	+2	+3
30. The Catholic belief system as a whole is...	-3	-2	-1	0	+1	+2	+3

V. Definition of the Church

    Introduction: Previously I asked you to indicate the thinking of
               the Church on various issues, with the qualification
               "as you define the Church." The following questions
               have to do with your definition and understanding of
               the Church.

1. How would you <u>define</u> the Catholic Church?

2. As you define it, is the Church primarily a visible (1)_____or
   invisible (5)_____organization?

                               (2) visible_____
   In between (do not suggest), but closer to (3) neither_____
                               (4) invisible_____

3. As you define it, is the Church primarily a divine (1)_____ or
   human (5)_____institution?

                               (2) divine_____
   In between (do not suggest), but closer to (3) neither_____
                               (4) human_____

4. In the concrete--as it <u>is</u>, not as it is defined--what is the
   Catholic Church? (if not answered above)

5. What image of the Church did you have in mind as you answered the
   list of beliefs?

6. Concretely, is the Church a rigid organization (1)_____, or a
   flexible one (5)_____?

                               (2) rigid_____
   In between (do not suggest), but closer to (3) neither_____
                               (4) flexible_____

7. Concretely, is the Church an organization with many schools of
   thought (1)_____, or one school of thought (5)_____?

                               (2) many schools_____
   In between (do not suggest), but closer to (3) neither_____
                               (4) one school_____

8. Concretely, is the Church a conservative organization (1)_____,
   or a liberal one (5)_____?

                                          (2) conservative_____
          In between (do not suggest), but closer to (3) neither_____
                                          (4) liberal_____

9. Concretely, is the Church an organization in which freedom of
   theological inquiry prevails (1)_____, or one in which dogma is
   passed down (5)_____?

                                          (2) freedom_____
          In between (do not suggest), but closer to (3) neither_____
                                          (4) dogma_____

10. Concretely, is the Church an organization that controls con-
    sciences (1)_____, or that creates free consciences (5)_____?

                                          (2) controls_____
          In between (do not suggest), but closer to (3) neither_____
                                          (4) creates free_____

11. Concretely, is the Church an organization involved in this world
    (1)_____, or directed to the next (5)_____?

                                          (2) this world_____
          In between (do not suggest), but closer to (3) neither_____
                                          (4) next world_____

12. Concretely, is the Church a bureaucratized hierarchy (1)_____, or
    a community of individuals (5)_____?

                                          (2) bur. hierarchy____
          In between (do not suggest), but closer to (3) neither_____
                                          (4) community ind.____

13. <u>Who</u> is the Catholic Church?

14. Who is at its core?

15. Who is at its periphery?

16.   Who is midway between core and periphery?

17.   Where is the power (in general) in the Catholic Church?

18.   Who has the most power?

19.   Who has the least power?

                                    /

20.   Who has an intermediate amount of power?

21.   In whose hands is the development of doctrine in the Church?

22.   Who, primarily, is responsible for it (in the concrete)?

      (Get segment of membership):

23.   What is the source of the impetus for change in the Church?

      (Get segment of membership):

24. Where is the most resistance to it?

    (Get segment of membership):

25. What <u>should</u> the Catholic Church be?

26. Can it ever become that?

27. Do you have any power in helping bring that about?

28. OUTS ONLY: Would you have had any such power had you remained a member?

29. What is the change that is going on in the Church? Sum up your understanding of it in a sentence or two.

30. How does the change affect your status of being _____?
                                                   In or Out

31. Does it make you feel comfortable (1)_____or uneasy (5)_____ about being _____?
                           In or Out

                                              (2) comfortable_____
    In between (do not suggest), but closer to (3) neither_____
                                              (4) uneasy_____

32. IF ANYTHING BUT NEITHER: Why?

33. How <u>would</u> <u>you</u> <u>like</u> the change to end up?

34. What <u>would</u> <u>you</u> <u>like</u> to remain unchanged?

35. Overall, do you consider the change to be positive (1)_____, or
    negative (5)_____?

                                        (2) positive_____
    In between (do not suggest), but closer to (3) neither_____
                                        (4) negative_____

36. By what criteria do you consider yourself _____ the Church?
                                              In or Out of

37. INS ONLY: Is one of the criteria a matter of being baptized
    or not?

            (1) Yes_____
            (2) No_____

38. Is one of the criteria a matter of religious practice, e.g., of
    attending Mass or not, of going to Confession or Communion or not?

            (1) Yes_____
            (2) No_____

39. Is one of the criteria a matter of believing or not believing what
    the Church teaches?

            (1) Yes_____
            (2) No_____

40. Is one of the criteria a matter of moral practice, e.g., of fol-
    lowing or not the teaching of the Church with regard to birth
    control, extra-marital sex?

            (1) Yes_____
            (2) No_____

41. Could someone else believe what you believe, or do what you do,
    and still consider himself _____ the Church?
                               In or Out of

42. IF YES: They why do you consider yourself _____ the
                                               In or Out of
    Church? How are you different from that someone else?

43. How often do you attend Mass?_____

44. How often do you go to Confession?_____

45. How often do you receive Communion?_____

46. If a Catholic got a divorce and remarried, would you still con-
    sider him a member of the Church?

            (1) Yes_____
            (2) No_____
            (3) Depends on:_____

47. If a Catholic openly professed a belief in opposition to the
    official teaching of the Church, would you still consider him a
    member of the Church?

            (1) Yes_____
            (2) No_____
            (3) Depends on:_____

48. If a Catholic did not attend Mass for five years, would you still
    consider him a member of the Church?

            (1) Yes_____
            (2) No_____
            (3) Depends on:_____

49. If a Catholic were excommunicated from the Church, would you still
    consider him a member of the Church?

            (1) Yes_____
            (2) No_____
            (3) Depends on:_____

VI. <u>Attitudes toward early Religious Figures and Parents</u>

1. Did you have priests or religious instruct you in grammar school?

   (1) Yes_____which?_____
   (2) No_____

2. IF YES TO 1: In general, were they out for your good (1)_____,
or their own good (5)_____?

           (2) your good_____
In between (do not suggest), but closer to (3) neither_____
           (4) their good_____

3. IF YES TO 1: In general, were they distant from you (1)_____,
or close to you (5)_____?

           (2) distant_____
In between (do not suggest), but closer to (3) neither_____
           (4) close_____

4. IF YES TO 1: In general, were they intelligent in religious
matters (1)_____, or not very intelligent (5)_____?

           (2) intelligent_____
In between (do not suggest), but closer to (3) neither_____
           (4) not intelligent__

5. Did you have priests or religious instruct you in high school?

   (1) Yes_____which?_____
   (2) No_____

6. IF YES TO 5: In general, were they out for your good (1)_____,
or their own good (5)_____?

           (2) your good_____
In between (do not suggest), but closer to (3) neither_____
           (4) their good_____

7. IF YES TO 5: In general, were they distant from you (1)_____,
or close to you (5)_____?

           (2) distant_____
In between (do not suggest), but closer to (3) neither_____
           (4) close_____

8. IF YES TO 5: In general were they intelligent in religious
matters (1)_____, or not very intelligent (5)_____?

           (2) intelligent_____
In between (do not suggest), but closer to (3) neither_____
           (4) not intelligent___

9. Did you have priests or religious instruct you in college?

    (1) Yes_____which?_____
    (2) No_____

10. IF YES TO 9: In general were they out for your good (1)_____,
    or their own good (5)_____?

                                              (2) your good_____
    In between (do not suggest), but closer to (3) neither_____
                                              (4) their good_____

11. IF YES TO 9: In general, were they distant from you (1)_____,
    or close to you (5)_____?

                                              (2) distant_____
    In between (do not suggest), but closer to (3) neither_____
                                              (4) close_____

12. IF YES TO 9: In general, were they intelligent in religious
    matters (1)_____ or not very intelligent (5)_____?

                                              (2) intelligent_____
    In between (do not suggest), but closer to (3) neither_____
                                              (4) not intelligent__

Introduction: The following questions have to do with your parents.

13. What quality in your **mother** did you especially like or admire?
    (If more than one, have interviewee pick out the most important
    one.)

14. What quality did you especially dislike, or find not admirable?
    (If more than one, have interviewee pick out the most important
    one.)

15. What quality in your **father** did you especially like or admire?
    (If more than one, have interviewee pick out the most important
    one.)

16. What quality did you especially dislike, or find not admirable?
    (If more than one, have interviewee pick out the most important
    one.)

17. Which parent was more responsible for disciplining you?

        (1) Mother_____
        (5) Father_____

                                    (2) Mother_____
Both (do not suggest), but closer to (3) neither_____
                                    (4) Father_____

18. Which parent did you feel closer to (while you were in the home)?

        (1) Mother_____
        (2) Father_____

                                      (2) Mother_____
Both (do not suggest), but closer to (3) neither_____
                                    (4) Father_____

19. Was either parent away from home for a considerable period of time? Which, and for how long?

20. Would you characterize your mother by checking the appropriate space between the following pairs of adjectives? (Judgments should be "objective," i.e., as compared with people in general, not in comparison with father.)

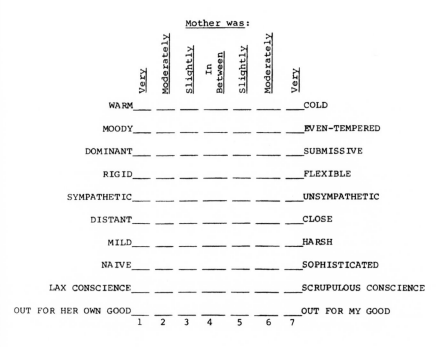

Mother was:

	Very	Moderately	Slightly	In Between	Slightly	Moderately	Very	
WARM	___	___	___	___	___	___	___	COLD
MOODY	___	___	___	___	___	___	___	EVEN-TEMPERED
DOMINANT	___	___	___	___	___	___	___	SUBMISSIVE
RIGID	___	___	___	___	___	___	___	FLEXIBLE
SYMPATHETIC	___	___	___	___	___	___	___	UNSYMPATHETIC
DISTANT	___	___	___	___	___	___	___	CLOSE
MILD	___	___	___	___	___	___	___	HARSH
NAIVE	___	___	___	___	___	___	___	SOPHISTICATED
LAX CONSCIENCE	___	___	___	___	___	___	___	SCRUPULOUS CONSCIENCE
OUT FOR HER OWN GOOD	___	___	___	___	___	___	___	OUT FOR MY GOOD
	1	2	3	4	5	6	7	

21. Would you characterize your father by checking the appropriate space between the following pairs of adjectives? (Judgments should be "objective," i.e., as compared with people in general, not in comparison with mother.)

Father was:

	Very	Moderately	Slightly	In Between	Slightly	Moderately	Very	
WARM	___	___	___	___	___	___	___	COLD
MOODY	___	___	___	___	___	___	___	EVEN-TEMPERED
DOMINANT	___	___	___	___	___	___	___	SUBMISSIVE
RIGID	___	___	___	___	___	___	___	FLEXIBLE
SYMPATHETIC	___	___	___	___	___	___	___	UNSYMPATHETIC
DISTANT	___	___	___	___	___	___	___	CLOSE
MILD	___	___	___	___	___	___	___	HARSH
NAIVE	___	___	___	___	___	___	___	SOPHISTICATED
LAX CONSCIENCE	___	___	___	___	___	___	___	SCRUPULOUS CONSCIENCE
OUT FOR HER OWN GOOD	___	___	___	___	___	___	___	OUT FOR MY GOOD
	1	2	3	4	5	6	7	

22. Is (was) your mother Catholic?

        (1) Yes_____
        (2) No_____

23. IF YES: Is (was) she a practicing Catholic (attendance at Sunday Mass 90% of the time)?

        (1) Yes_____
        (2) No_____

24. IF YES TO 22: Was she born a Catholic (1)_____, or was she a convert (2)_____?

25. Is (was) your father Catholic?

        (1) Yes_____
        (2) No_____

26. IF YES: Is (was) he a practicing Catholic (attendance at Sunday Mass 90% of the time)?

      (1) Yes_____
      (2) No_____

27. IF YES TO 25: Was he born a Catholic (1)_____, or was he a convert (2)_____?

28. What was your <u>mother's</u> attitude toward Catholicism?

29. Would you characterize it as: (Read categories.)

      (1)_____Strongly favorable
      (2)_____Favorable
      (3)_____Slightly favorable
      (4)_____Neutral
      (5)_____Slightly unfavorable
      (6)_____Unfavorable
      (7)_____Strongly unfavorable

30. Was she intelligent in religious matters (1)_____, or not very intelligent (5)_____?

                            (2) intelligent_____
In between (do not suggest), but closer to (3) neither_____
                            (4) not intelligent___

31. What was your father's attitude toward Catholicism?

32. Would you characterize it as: (Read categories.)

      (1)_____Strongly favorable
      (2)_____Favorable
      (3)_____Slightly favorable
      (4)_____Neutral
      (5)_____Slightly unfavorable
      (6)_____Unfavorable
      (7)_____Strongly unfavorable

33. Was he intelligent in religious matters (1)_____, or not very intelligent (5)_____?

                                          (2) intelligent_____
    In between (do not suggest), but closer to (3) neither_____
                                          (4) not intelligent___

34. Which parent's attitude was more strongly favorable toward Catholicism?

                (1) Mother_____
                (5) Father_____

                                          (2) Mother_____
    In between (do not suggest), but closer to (3) neither_____
                                          (4) Father_____

35. Did they see eye to eye on Catholicism (1)_____, or did they disagree about it (5)_____?

                                          (2) eye to eye_____
    In between (do not suggest), but closer to (3) neither_____
                                          (4) disagree_____

VII. Demographic Items

1. Sex: (1) Male_____
            (2) Female_____

2. Age: (1) 21 and under_____
          (2) 22_____
          (3) 23_____
          (4) 24_____
          (5) 25_____
          (6) 26_____
          (7) 27_____
          (8) 28_____
          (9) 29 and over (specify):_____

3. Highest degree attained in school: (1) bachelor's_____
                                         (2) master's___in:_____
                                         (3) professional___specify:____

                                         (4) Ph.D.___in:_____

4. Occupation:_____if student, year in school:_____

5. Average annual income (if married, family income):

                         (1) under $5,000_____
                         (2) $5,001 to $7,500_____
                         (3) $7,501 to $10,000_____
                         (4) $10,001 to $12,500_____
                         (5) $12,501 to $15,000_____
                         (6) over $15,000_____

6. Marital status: (1) single_____
                    (2) married, living with spouse_____
                    (3) married, separated from spouse_____
                    (4) divorced_____
                    (5) widowed_____

7. Number of children: (0)_____ (1)_____ (2)_____ (3)_____ (4)_____

                      (5)_____ (6)_____ (7)_____ (8)_____ (9)_____

                      or more than 9_____

8. Spouse's religion: (1) Catholic_____
                     (2) other_____specify:_____

                    Was he (she) ever Catholic?_____

9. Spouse's occupation:_____

10. Mother's education--highest level attained:

           (1)_____graduate grammar school
           (2)_____graduate high school
           (3)_____graduate college
           (4)_____master's degree
           (5)_____professional degree
           (6)_____Ph.D.

11. Mother's occupation (major):_____
                                  (indicate if housewife)

12. Mother's ethnic background:_____

13. Was she born in the United States?   (1) Yes_____
                                          (2) No_____

14. Father's education--highest level attained:

             (1)_____graduate grammar school
             (2)_____graduate high school
             (3)_____graduate college
             (4)_____master's degree
             (5)_____professional degree
             (6)_____Ph.D.

15. Father's occupation (major):_____

16. Father's ethnic background:_____

17. Was he born in the United States: (1) Yes_____
                                         (2) No_____

18. Your own birthplace:_____

19. Family income (average annual, when subject was 15):

             (1) under $5,000_____
             (2) $5,001 to $10,000_____
             (3) $10,001 to $15,000_____
             (4) $15,001 to $20,000_____
             (5) $20,001 to $25,000_____
             (6) over $25,000_____

20. How many brothers_____and sisters_____do you have?

                  * * * * * * * * * * * * * * *

A. Why were you willing to be a subject in this survey?

B. What do you think is my status with regard to Catholicism?

    (a) In (1)_____or Out (2)_____or never Catholic (3)_____?

    (b) IF IN: Liberal (1)_____or (2) Conservative_____?

Time completed:_____

VIII.   Interviewer Evaluation Sheet

1. Any outstanding impressions of the subject:

2. Was he honest and open in the interview?

3. Description of setting of interview:

4. Hypotheses to consider in this study as a whole:

Bibliography

Allport, G. W., J. M. Gillespie, and J. Young. The religion of the post-war college student. *J. Psychol.*, 1948, *25*, 3–33.

Allport, G. W., P. E. Vernon, and G. Lindzey. *A Study of Values: A Scale for Measuring the Dominant Interests in Personality* (3d ed.). Boston: Houghton Mifflin, 1960.

Aronfreed, Justin. The nature, variety, and social patterning of moral responses to transgression. *J. Abnorm. Soc. Psychol.*, 1961, *63*, 223–240.

Asch, Solomon E. Forming impressions of personality. *J. Abnorm. Soc. Psychol.*, 1946, *41*, 258–290.

———. Studies of independence and conformity: a minority of one against a unanimous majority. *Psychol. Monogr.*, 1956, *70*, No. 9 (Whole No. 416).

Baldwin, Alfred. *Theories of Child Development*. New York: John Wiley and Sons, 1967.

Bandura, Albert and Aletha C. Huston. Identification as a process of incidental learning. *J. Abnorm. Soc. Psychol.*, 1961, *63*, 311–318.

Bandura, Albert, Dorothea Ross, and Sheila Ross. A comparative test of the status envy, social power, and secondary reinforcement theories of identification learning. *J. Abnorm. Soc. Psychol.*, 1963, *67*, 527–534.

Barry, Herbert, Margaret K. Bacon, and Irvin L. Child. A cross-cultural survey of some sex differences in socialization. *J. Abnorm. Soc. Psychol.*, 1957, *55*, 327–332.

Baum, Gregory. *The Credibility of the Church Today: A Reply to Charles Davis*. New York: Herder and Herder, 1968.

261

Becker Research Corporation. *The Impact of Vatican II: A Survey of the Laity in the Diocese of Worcester.* Boston, 1969.

Berry, J. L. and B. Martin. GSR reactivity as a function of anxiety, instructions, and sex. *J. Abnorm. Soc. Psychol.,* 1957, *54,* 9–12.

Callahan, Daniel. *The New Church.* New York: Scribner, 1966.

Clark, Kenneth B. *Dark Ghetto: Dilemmas of Social Power.* New York: Harper and Row, 1965.

D'Andrade, Roy G. Sex differences and cultural institutions. In Eleanor Maccoby, (ed.), *The Development of Sex Differences.* Stanford: Stanford University Press, 1966.

Davis, Charles. *A Question of Conscience.* New York: Harper and Row, 1967.

Elkind, David and Sally Elkind. Varieties of religious experience in young adolescents. *J. Scient. St. Rel.,* 1962, *2,* 102–112.

Ellis, John Tracey. American Catholics and the intellectual life. *Thought,* 1955 (Autumn), *30.*

Fogarty, Michael P. *Christian Democracy in Western Europe.* London: Routledge and Kegan Paul, 1957.

Greeley, Andrew M. The Protestant Ethic: Time for a moratorium. *Sociol. Anal.,* 1964, *25,* 20–33.

———. The religious behavior of graduate students. *J. Scient. St. Rel.,* 1965, *5,* 34–40.

———. *The Catholic Experience.* New York: Doubleday & Co., 1967.

———. *A Future to Hope In.* New York: Doubleday & Co., 1969.

Greeley, Andrew M. and Peter H. Rossi. *The Education of Catholic Americans.* Chicago: Aldine, 1966.

Grusec, Joan and Walter Mischel. Model's characteristics as determinants of social learning. *J. Pers. Soc. Psychol.,* 1966, *4,* 211–215.

Hamburg, David A. and Donald T. Lunde. Sex hormones in the development of sex differences in human behavior. In Eleanor Maccoby (ed.), *The Development of Sex Differences.* Stanford: Stanford University Press, 1966.

Hampson, J. and Joan Hampson. The ontogenesis of sexual behavior in man. In W. C. Young (ed.), *Sex and Internal Secretions.* Baltimore: Williams and Wilkins, 1961.

Henderson, Bruce. Catholic freedom vs. authority. *Time,* November 22, 1968, 42–49.

Hoffman, Martin L. Childrearing practices and moral development: Generalizations from empirical research. *Child Development,* 1963, *34,* 295–318.

Hoffman, Martin L. and Herbert D. Saltzstein. Parent discipline and the child's moral development. *J. Pers. Soc. Psychol.*, 1967, *5*, 45–57.

Hyman, H. H. *Interviewing in Social Research.* Chicago: The University of Chicago Press, 1954.

Kagan, Jerome and Howard Moss. *Birth to Maturity.* New York: John Wiley and Sons, 1962.

Kahn, R. L. and C. F. Cannell. *The Dynamics of Interviewing.* New York: John Wiley and Sons, 1957.

Kavanaugh, James. *A Modern Priest Looks at His Outdated Church.* New York: Trident Press, 1967.

Kelley, Harold H. The warm-cold variable in first impressions of persons. *J. Person.*, 1950, *18*, 431–439.

Kohlberg, Lawrence. Moral development and identification. In H. Stevenson (ed.), *Child Psychology: Sixty-Second Yearbook of the National Society for the Study of Education.* Chicago: The University of Chicago Press, 1963.

———. The development of moral character and ideology. In M. Hoffman and L. Hoffman (eds.), *Review of Child Development Research,* Vol. I. New York: Russell Sage, 1964.

———. A cognitive-developmental analysis of children's sex-role concepts and attitudes. In Eleanor Maccoby (ed.), *The Development of Sex Differences.* Stanford: Stanford University Press, 1966.

Kung, Hans. *Freedom Today.* New York: Sheed and Ward, 1966.

———. *The Church.* New York: Sheed and Ward, 1968.

Lansky, L. M., V. J. Crandall, J. Kagan, and C. T. Baker. Sex differences in aggression and its correlates in middle-class adolescents. *Child Develpm.*, 1961, *32*, 45–58.

Lazerwitz, Bernard. Religion and social structure in the United States. In Louis Schneider (ed.), *Religion, Culture, and Society: A Reader in the Sociology of Religion.* New York: John Wiley and Sons, 1964.

Maccoby, Eleanor E. (ed.) *The Development of Sex Differences.* Stanford: Stanford University Press, 1966.

MacKinnon, D. W. Violation and prohibitions. In H. A. Murray (ed.), *Explorations in Personality.* New York: Oxford University Press, 1938.

McCord, W. and Joan McCord. *Psychopathy and Delinquency.* New York: Grune and Stratton, 1956.

McKenzie, John L., S. J. *Authority in the Church.* New York: Sheed and Ward, 1966.

Mischel, Walter. A social-learning view of sex differences in behavior. In Eleanor Maccoby (ed.), *The Development of Sex Differences*. Stanford: Stanford University Press, 1966.

O'Dea, Thomas. *American Catholic Dilemma*. New York: Sheed and Ward, 1958.

Rosen, Bernard C. and Roy D'Andrade. The psychosocial origins of achievement motivation. *Sociometry*, 1959, *22*, 185–195.

Rosenberg, Milton J. Cognitive structure and attitudinal affect. *J. Abnorm. Soc. Psychol.*, 1956, *53*, 367–372.

————. Cognitive reorganization in response to the hypnotic reversal of attitudinal affect. *J. Person.*, 1960, *28*, 39–63.

Rosenthal, Robert. *Experimenter Effects in Behavioral Research*. New York: Appleton-Century-Crofts, 1966.

Ruether, Rosemary. *The Church against Itself*. New York: Herder and Herder, 1968.

Schneider, Louis (ed.). *Religion, Culture, and Society: A Reader in the Sociology of Religion*. New York: John Wiley and Sons, 1964.

Sears, R. R., E. Maccoby, and H. Levin. *Patterns of Child Rearing*. Evanston, Ill.: Row, Peterson, 1957.

Sears, R. R., Lucy Rau, and R. Alpert. *Identification and Child Rearing*. Stanford: Stanford University Press, 1965.

Sherif, Muzafer. *The Psychology of Social Norms*. New York: Harper and Row, 1936.

Solomon, R. L., L. J. Kamin, and L. C. Wynne. Traumatic avoidance learning: The outcomes of several extinction procedures with dogs. *J. Abnorm. Soc. Psychol.*, 1953, *48*, 291–302.

Sontag, L. W. Physiological factors and personality in children. *Child Develpm.*, 1947, *18*, 185–189.

Suenens, Leo Cardinal. *Co-responsibility in the Church*. New York: Herder and Herder, 1968.

Teilhard de Chardin, Pierre. *The Phenomenon of Man*. New York: Harper and Row, 1959.

Whiting, J. W. M. Resource mediation and learning by identification. In I. Iscoe and H. W. Stevenson (eds.), *Personality Development in Children*. Austin: University of Texas Press, 1960.

Witkin, H. A., R. B. Dyk, F. H. Faterson, D. R. Goodenough, and S. A. Karp. *Psychological Differentiation*. New York: John Wiley and Sons, 1962.

Index

Religious practice, *see* Practice
Revolution, 15–16, 33, 109, 195–198
Rising expectations, *see* Expectations
Rosen, B., 163
Rosenberg, M., 74–75
Rosenthal, R., 14
Rossi, P. H., 23, 132

Sacraments, 33–34, 36, 50, 93, 132, 167
   see also Confession, Eucharist, Mass
Saltzstein, H., 160
Sears, R., 160
Sex
   behavior, 46, 175
   beliefs regarding, 47, 58, 61–62, 64–65, 67, 69
   differences, 8, 121–140, 142–144, 165, 173, 175–176
      in beliefs, 9, 121–124, 126–127, 131–132, 134–135, 140, 170
      in change processes, 9, 121, 125–126, 137
      in demographic characteristics, 22, 121–125
      in overall religious characteristics, 126, 131–134, 136–137, 139–140, 142, 170, 173, 181
      in perceptions of the Church, 9, 121–124, 128–132, 134, 138, 140
      in psychological characteristics, 121, 133–140, 170
      in values, 9, 121, 124, 127–128, 132
   influence between the sexes, 36, 41, 44, 46–49, 126, 135, 142, 170–171
   relationship to membership status, 9, 170, 175–176
   values regarding, 77, 79–80, 82, 85–86
   see also Identification with parents (same-sex and cross-sex factors in), Parents (relationship to status of children)
Sherif, M., 171
Sin, 32, 35, 46, 60–61, 63, 66–67, 69, 78, 85, 102, 124
Solomon, R., 136
Sontag, L., 136
Statistics, 199–201
Subjects, 10–28, 186, 190
   demographic information on, 4, 9, 15–18, 28
   representativeness of, 23–24 132–133, 184–185, 196–197, 199–201
   source of, 11, 21–23, 27
   see also Education of subjects, Sex differences in demographic characteristics

Teilhard de Chardin, P., 32, 187
"Thinking of the Church," *see* Catholic Church (beliefs of)
Threat in the Church, 195–198

Unitarians, 39

Values, 4, 5, 9, 15–16, 73–90, 93, 127, 158, 162, 166, 179
   measurement of, 74–76
   see also Allport-Vernon-Lindzey Study of Values, Membership as instrumental in value fulfillment, Sex differences in values, Sex (values regarding)
Voluntary organization, Church as, 195–198

Whiting, J., 159
Witkin, H., 137

Printed in the United States
220061BV00001B/20/P

9 780202 363073